Adventures with the First Municipal Park Naturalist
at Lake Merritt, America's Oldest Waterfowl Refuge

People Are
for the Birds

Paul F. Covel

DRAWINGS BY NANCY CLEMENT

Western Interpretive Press ❧ *Oakland, California*

The frontispiece photo was taken by R.L. Copeland and is used through the courtesy of the Oakland Chamber of Commerce. In the foreground is the Waterfowl Refuge and Duck Islands on Oakland's Lake Merritt. Behind Lakeside Park is downtown Oakland, California, and in the background can be seen the Bay Bridge and the city of San Francisco, with the Pacific Ocean in the far distance.

Paul F. Covel

People Are for the Birds

Contents

Photographs

Foreword

*I*t is unusual for a person who has devoted his life to interpretation of the wonders of nature to find the time to put his observations and activities into book form. Mr. Paul Covel, who was for twenty-eight years the naturalist at Lakeside Park's Wildlife Refuge, has accomplished that feat. His dry sense of humor, keen observation of the habits of animals and people comes across in his book clearly and makes for delightful reading.

For the professional naturalist the book provides an ample number of stories and observation of the birds and animals that inhabit Lakeside Park and Lake Merritt that will be of great interest to a person studying the subject. Mr. Covel's discussion of the trials and tribulations of establishing a nature center and an interpretive program in an urban center will be of significant value to anyone planning such a development.

For the lay person the book provides a fascinating story of a naturalist's struggle to bring to an urban population an understanding of its relationship to the environment and the wildlife that exists. Throughout the book Mr. Covel presents facets of Oakland's history and the background of the interpretive movement which makes for interesting, educational and enjoyable reading.

William Penn Mott, Jr.

November, 1977

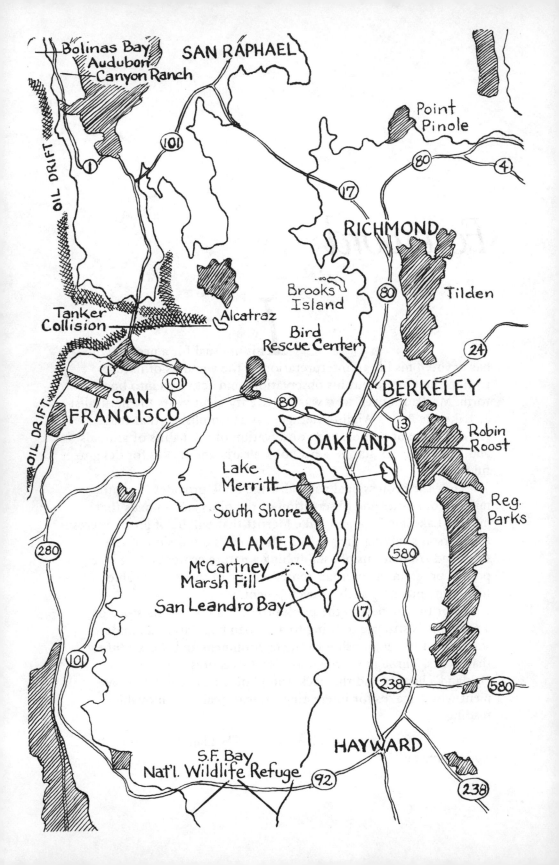

Acknowledgments

This book is dedicated to my wife—Marion—who enjoyed and endured many of these adventures with me and who has done yeoman work on this manuscript.

I am indebted to the many persons who read, commented or counseled on this manuscript. Special thanks are due Phillip and Anne Arend, James F. Covel, Susan Frugé, Harlan Kessel, Frederick J. Monteagle and Glenn and Pat Taylor, and to the Oakland Office of Parks and Recreation for certain of the photographs, and to Bill Parsons for the nesting goose photo. The aerial view frontispiece came from the files of the Oakland Chamber of Commerce.

P. F. C.

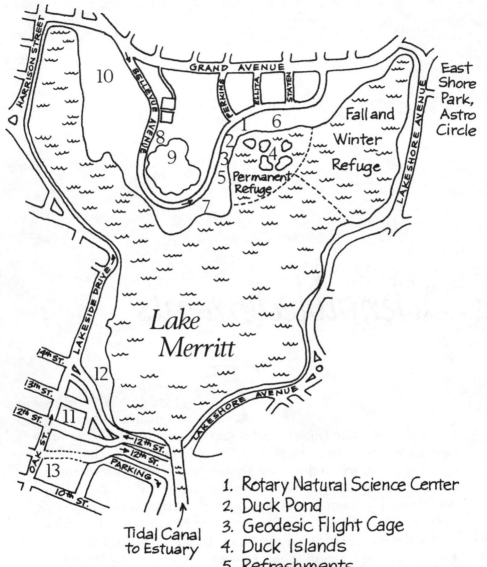

HARRISON STREET

BELLEVUE AVENUE

GRAND AVENUE

PERKINS
ELITA
STATEN

East
Shore
Park,
Astro
Circle

LAKESHORE AVENUE

10

8

9

1
2
3
5
7

6
4

Fall and
Winter
Refuge

Permanent
Refuge

Lake
Merritt

LAKESIDE DRIVE

14th ST.

13th ST.

12th ST.

12

OAK ST.

11

13

LAKESHORE AVENUE

12th ST.

12th ST.

PARKING

10th ST.

7

Tidal Canal
to Estuary

1. Rotary Natural Science Center
2. Duck Pond
3. Geodesic Flight Cage
4. Duck Islands
5. Refreshments
6. Play Area
7. Sailboat House: Boat Storage
   and Launching
8. Lakeside Park Garden Center
9. Nurseries, Trial & Show Gardens
10. Children's Fairyland
11. Alameda County Court House
12. Old Oakland Public Museum
13. New Oakland Museum

Lake Merritt, the First Wildlife Refuge

The Big Man smiled as he tossed another handful of crusts to his ducks. An enormous brown and white mottled drake was out in front as usual, snatching the biggest pieces for himself. The purebred mallard drakes with shiny green heads and white collars and their plain brown hens crowded as close behind as they dared. Several snowy-breasted pintail and their plain slender mates hovered expectantly a few feet farther off-shore. Like the canvasback and scaup which floated far out on the lake, the pintail or sprig were fall migrants which had to establish their rights and privileges among the fat, bossy mallards, Pekins, and hybrids which lived here the year-round.

The Big Man had good reason to feel complacent and charitable toward these birds and the world in general. He was Dr. Samuel Merritt, recently elected mayor of Oakland. His palatial

1

home overlooked the sprawling, marsh-bordered lake and across
a lovely oak-studded terrain toward the sun-baked hills topped by
a thin fringe of redwoods. To the west, it was only a few blocks
to the heart of Oakland's booming business district, but business
establishments and apartment houses in 1869 had not yet intruded
on the pastoral atmosphere of the lake shore. The few other lakeside dwellers had their own boat piers and some enterprising fellow
was renting rowboats to fishermen and picnickers—some of whom
came all the way from San Francisco on the "creek ferry." A
Catholic convent and high school had just been established not
too far away on the northwest arm of the lake.

Coast Miwok Indians had stalked the waterfowl around these
same shores just a few decades earlier and set nets for the ducks.
Black-tailed deer and herds of elk had splashed into these same
marsh fringes when the monstrous grizzlies charged them as they
pastured under the live oaks. In 1772, explorers Lieutenant Pedro
Fages and Padre Crespi described this savage setting when they
finally penetrated this far along the "Contra Costa" side of San
Francisco Bay and paused to celebrate Mass on the shores of the
north arm of this estuary.

This land was left in undisputed possession of its Indian
occupants for another four decades until the Mexican governor
of Alta California in 1820 gave eleven leagues (44,800 acres) of it
to a faithful soldier, Sergeant Maria Luis Peralta. Peralta's son,
Antonio, a few years later was given the huge slice of this grant
which would later become the cities of Oakland and Alameda.
But this small empire was soon wrested from Antonio's hands by
ambitious, scheming Yankee settlers and developers. The Peraltas,
their cattle and vaqueros, like the Indians and grizzlies, were soon
erased ruthlessly from the scene.

But the forces of Nature remained to challenge and to plague
the new masters of what was known as "Laguna Peralta," this
vast inland tidal slough. Twice each day low tides exposed acres
of unsightly and often smelly mud flat. Private sewer lines ran into
this convenient, common cesspool, and it was most unpleasant
to be reminded of this at each low tide.

The Big Man, Dr. Merritt, as the new mayor of Oakland,
offered a solution to this vexing situation. He offered to personally supply the plans and lumber, and supervise construction of a
wide, earthen dam on the tidal canal, together with a new roadway.

2

This structure would replace the crude toll-bridge built there a few years earlier by the enterprising Horace W. Carpentier, and would create a permanent recreation lake for Oakland. The city council agreed. After all, who could argue against a Mayor who stood six feet three in height, tipped the scales at 340 pounds, and was a powerful professional and political figure? The ultimate cost of this project to the city—some $20,000—had shaken the treasury and the Honorable Councilmen so badly that he, Samuel Merritt, hadn't bothered to present a few bills he had personally paid to get his dam finished! Some citizens were already beginning to call it "Lake Merritt," which naturally was not unpleasant to the Big Man's ears.

Shots heard across the country

The Big Man glanced skyward just in time to note a formation of new ducks gliding down toward his shoreline when "wham— bang—whoosh," blasted out some shotguns in the morning stillness. The shots sounded very close—maybe even on his lakeshore frontage. Two of the incoming ducks folded their wings and went into a dizzy spin, crashing into the tule growth out of the Mayor's sight.

"Hey, get out of there, you damn poachers," yelled the Big Man in his most stentorian, menacing voice. "You're trespassing. I'll have the constable on you!"

The sounds of retreating splashes and brushing of the tules was the mayor's only reply. Some of the ducks he had been feeding, like their wild brethren in the background, were already winging out toward the safer, open water of mid lake.

The Big Man laboriously made his way back toward the mansion on the hill. He looked very grim and was muttering to himself. He vowed to take immediate action against these poachers. Why only last week a shotgun charge had lodged in the backside of his neighbor's cow, and the week before a rifle slug had crashed through his—the Mayor's—own bedroom window. Now he had an idea. He would present it to the very next council meeting. Why, these first poachers' shots might be the ones heard around the world!

Mayor Merritt kept his promise to himself and to his ducks. He didn't merely ask the city fathers to draw up another ordinance —one that would prohibit all hunting and shooting around their new lake. With his considerable persuasion, tact, and position as Mayor, he talked State Senator Edward Thompson into introducing in the state legislature a bill to create thereon a "State Waterfowl Refuge." Under California law the state had retained title to this "tidal lake," in spite of the avaricious schemes of various developers.

The Great Event took place on March 18, 1870. Governor Henry Haight signed Senator Thompson's bill, which had been passed by the legislature. Now Oakland possessed the first wildlife refuge to be declared by any legislative body in North America! I doubt many of the citizens realized what fame and distinction this would eventually bring to the city. There was still no public park and no public road around the lake, and poachers continued to sneak through the marshy fringes and bag a few birds.

But Lake Merritt, as it soon became known officially, remained the only declared public wildlife refuge in North America until 1903, when President Theodore Roosevelt set aside Pelican Island, off the coast of Florida, as a federal refuge. Was it the Lake Merritt example that inspired Roosevelt, the Conservationist, to dare try this federal experiment—and to follow it with a string of other refuges across the nation? Those shots that moved the mayor to demand a state refuge may well have reverberated across the continent.

The people of Oakland and their visitors finally enjoyed a public park on Lake Merritt. It was won only after years of bitter political feuds and open warfare. Big business and many local entrepreneurs fought desperately to retain their holds on the Lake, as well as on all of Oakland's waterfront. The will of the people finally prevailed, and during Mayor Frank Mott's administration, they voted nearly a million dollars to buy and develop park lands. Around the same live oaks that had sheltered Indians, elk, and grizzlies, and later the Peraltas' herds, were planted trees and shrubs from many lands, as well as native trees transplanted from the hills and coastline, to create magnificent Lakeside Park.

The wild ducks and many other kinds of waterfowl continued to drop in for the fall and winter months. The descendants of the mallards fed by Mayor Merritt thrived and multiplied. Park visitors brought food for them and a few sympathetic city gardeners shared their lunches with the birds. The gardeners even provided fresh water troughs for the ducks which would leave their saltwater lake for fresh water baths and drinks.

Feeding birds with taxpayers' money

Then came a Day of Disaster in 1915. An oil slick from ships in the Estuary washed through the tidal canal when the flood gates were open, and with it a tragic, oil-soaked lot of canvasbacks and other deepwater, diving ducks. It was a prelude to the greater disasters of oil slicks which would imperil waterfowl in later years—from Lake Merritt to coasts around the world.

A loud public outcry demanded some official action to save these ducks. From what little can be found on this incident, it is doubtful that many of these birds were actually caught and cleaned. But the ducks that survived obviously needed help in the form of food. The city council in a grand gesture of pity and generosity authorized the park commission to buy grain for these starving ducks. Here again, history was made at Lake Merritt. Wild waterfowl were put on a dole from public funds! As a matter of fact, we suspect that far more of the resident mallards, dumped Pekins, and other unwanted paddle-footed pets benefited much more on a year-round basis than the real migrants. But a tradition was established and public opinion would never allow the city fathers to cut off the ducks' official free meals, though this was attempted more than once when park budgets ran short.

As more and more tourists, roving reporters, and photographers spread the story of these wild ducks feeding from citizens'
hands, or foraging on the park lawns which lakeshore residents
regarded as their front yards, the fame and prestige of Lake Merritt
and of Oakland grew. The mayor, city council, park commission,
and the chamber of commerce each and all claimed their full
share of glory for promoting this municipal attraction. It received
far more publicity outside of Oakland than the races and regattas
on the lake or the dance festivals and other cultural affairs staged
in Lakeside Park.

A new mayor and administration had taken over before
World War I. Mayor John Davie, a flamboyant, old-west type of
figure, was determined to "do something for those ducks" just as
substantial as his rival and predecessor, Frank Mott. A large amount
of earth fill was available as the new civic auditorium was constructed on the far side of the lake. Mayor Davie announced that his
workers would construct "an island for the birds" some distance
offshore from the feeding beach. A large, shallow, fresh-water
pool and fountain had just been built a short way from shore, protected by a low fence for the visitors who came to feed and to
watch the waterfowl cavort in this new facility.

"Build an island for those damn ducks?" cried some of the
Mayor's political enemies. "What a waste of public funds! Why
can't they nest in Lakeside Park as they always have?"

But John Davie was a stubborn fellow once he had adopted
a project or a cause. The mighty Southern Pacific Railroad learned
this to their sorrow when they tried to put his five cent "creek
ferry" on the Estuary out of business. His crews went right ahead
forming a small "Duck Island" as the loads of fill were barged
across the lake. The mayor had even ordered that a fresh water
line be laid from shore to irrigate the trees and shrubs being planted and to keep a small drinking and bathing basin for the birds!

The political hecklers named it "Davie's Folly," but the ducks
didn't care—nor did the mayor. The opportunist mallards eagerly
staked out nesting sites when the island opened for occupancy
in 1925. That fall the bird-watchers pointed out that the shyer,
just-arrived migrants—some of the pintail and widgeon—flocked
ashore on "Davie's Island" for free drinks from the fresh water
trough. This helped to hold these newcomers on the refuge until
they learned of the free meals offered along shore and at the Duck

6

Feeding Station, or overcame their natural wariness enough to mingle with humans.

Ducks and boats don't mix

Next, the mayor, the Lakeside Park gardeners, the bird-feeders and bird-watchers noted with alarm the growing conflict between the several thousands of migrant waterfowl arriving each fall and the weekend pleasure-boat sailors who invaded this north-east arm of the lake where the birds preferred to feed and loaf. Ducks and boats just didn't mix, particularly the canvasback, scaup, ruddy and other divers who fed off the bottom or took handouts from the bank, but positively refused to venture ashore. Every time a boat moved into their private waters, they rose with a great clatter and a few verbal protests and took off for San Francisco Bay, though a few smarter birds might just settle out on the broad main part of the lake until the invaders departed.

This was an intolerable situation, agreed the mayor and his council. These fall-winter migrants which had brought such fame to Oakland must have a refuge in fact as well as in name and legal standing. So they passed an ordinance setting aside the entire northeast arm of Lake Merritt as a waterfowl refuge from October to April. Then the mayor ordered the park department to come up with some plan to exclude all boating from that area.

The solution was a log barrier, also called a boom. Such a boom was built and one October day was towed across the north-east arm just beyond the new Duck Island. Some of the pleasure-boaters grumbled and protested for awhile, but the boom stayed.

The waterfowl reacted to their new, private and exclusive domain by increasing their flocks by hundreds. The jittery but easily decoyed or deluded canvasbacks gathered to the total of two thousand or more by mid-November. Albert Thomas and Cleve Norris, the Lakeside employees long responsible for the birds' care and welfare, took turns trudging along the shore to the historic Embarcadero side, at the apex of the northeast arm, where a grain locker had been established. The same soft "postman's whistle" used at the main feeding place was blown here. Canvas-backs by the hundreds came swarming in, accompanied by lesser numbers of scaups and ruddies and a few mooching mallards. Soon the water and bottom silt were churning like a maelstrom as the ducks alternately worked the bottom for the grain and emerged

7

for air. Scores of citizens and tourists followed the caretakers from the main feeding station or met them at the Embarcadero to marvel at the spectacle.

Mayor Davie had another great innovation — an historic "first" for Lake Merritt and for Oakland. We cannot say that he conceived this sensational new program, but he certainly accepted it, won its approval by the city council, and authorized the oft-shaken park commission and the park superintendent to spend some city funds to get it launched.

"What? Round up those foolish ducks and put tags on them? What will that crazy John Davie want to do next?" Some of the comments of the political carpers must have sounded something like that, but unfortunately we can't find them in print.

This was no wild experiment, however. The United States Biological Survey had found a local "cooperator" who would volunteer to band, report, and faithfully keep records on the Lake Merritt ducks — and any other waterfowl that should be banded. This would establish another vital link in the chain of bird-banding stations that the Survey, under the direction of the brilliant Frederick C. Lincoln, was stringing across the country.

The new "cooperator" was E.W. Ehman, a wealthy business man and avid sportsman, who lived in the nearby community of Piedmont. How effectively and completely this dedicated man carried out his unpaid assignment and how the Lake Merritt duck-banding initiated in 1926 became a popular institution will be told in a later chapter. Let us simply say that the band recoveries and long distance records which soon resulted were so rewarding that few of the Mayor's critics ever dared call this program another of His Honor's "damn fool tax-spending notions."

Nature Man Makes the Scene

The story of the Lake Merritt Waterfowl Refuge might have been a very different one if it hadn't been for several "nature men." Pioneer in the radical (then visionary) idea of a "park naturalist" for Oakland was "Bugs" Cain, really Brighton C. Cain. The Oakland Boy Scout Council had unwittingly stamped themselves as progressives when they hired this eager young naturalist, just out of Stanford, after trying him out at their Sierra Nevada summer camp. Bugs immediately established himself in a shack, soon to be known as the "Bug House," at the Council's beautiful in-town "Camp Dimond" in the pines and cypresses of the Oakland Hills. Boys flocked to this "nature man" who could all in a day introduce birds, botany, insects, astronomy, and informal lessons in philosophy and behavior. Scouts followed him on countless "merit badge preparation hikes," which regularly included Lakeside Park and bird study on Lake Merritt.

Bugs Cain soon formed a small circle of his most dedicated and accomplished bird students, though he remained teacher, advisor, father-confessor to all his boys. This very special club adopted the name: Oakland Ornithological Club. Some of its members were to become recognized naturalists, scientists, and professors.

The Oakland Ornithological Club's first tangible contribution to the bird-watchers of Oakland and like-minded visitors was to print and distribute a list, "The Birds of Lake Merritt and Lakeside Park." This pamphlet listed the carefully authenticated names of 138 waterfowl and land birds.

Guiding his boys through this publishing venture was a breakthrough for Bugs in his one-man campaign to impress the city fathers that they had a rare opportunity for conservation education in the Lake Merritt Waterfowl Refuge. A man of intense curiosity about natural things, who had the ability to communicate this to others—even to some lethargic grownups—Cain became fired with the possibilities for education in the wealth of variety of plantings in Lakeside and other city parks, and in the fauna and flora along the trails in Oakland's hill parks. He had already brought Boy Scouts to participate in every duck roundup and banding since he took the scout post. He was well known as "that nature man with the boys" by every park employee up to the superintendent, and to some of the commissioners and city councilmen as well.

Bugs Cain never asked for a dollar from the city, or from any church, club, or school he entertained in addition to his heavy scouting demands. It was generally thought he drew on some private income beyond his modest scout salary to buy books, cameras, field glasses, and many other things he loaned to trusted followers.

Finally, the superintendent of parks, Lee Kerfoot, and some of the commissioners decided they had to give this nature man some official recognition. Cain appeared in so many parks and greeted so many citizens and tourists that he came to act as an unofficial ranger-naturalist, public answer-man, and, on some occasions, the figure in uniform who sternly rebuked tree-choppers, fire-starters, or boys with b-b guns.

The Superintendent summoned Cain to his comfortable executive suite high in the Oakland City Hall and made the presentation. It was a plain tin star, but it bore those magic words: "Naturalist, Oakland Park Department."* No salary accompanied

*In 1968, the Oakland Park Department was merged with the Recreation Department and this facility is now known as the Office of Parks and Recreation.

10

this honorary office, but it may well have been the very first such title bestowed by any municipal park system in the United States. Bugs was most appreciative.

About 1931 I entered the scene. I was an avid bird watcher, scientific collector, and student of trees, shrubs, and almost anything else that appealed to me. I fell under the spell of Bugs Cain. In fact, I made up a considerable number of bird and mammal study skins for him—the kind that were laid out neatly in Bugs' skin cabinet at the Bug House, each with a proper label.

"Please don't go out and shoot a shrike, Paul," Bugs would say, "but I sure need one for the collection if anybody picks one up."

In those depression years, we needed regular meals, a modest rent, and gasoline for any field trips we could scrounge. Bugs paid hard cash for any prepared specimen he needed for his teaching collection. "Forgive me, dear friend," I can say now, "I did help a lot of those birds and mammals to become specimen material!" But perhaps Bugs really suspected it all the time.

Bugs' unquenchable enthusiasm rubbed off on me. I joined the Lake Merritt bird-watchers and also scoured every acre of Lakeside and other city parks until I thought I knew every tree, shrub, and flower—both native and exotic—complete to their Latin names and classifications. The gardeners and the foremen were sympathetic and generous with their information. I often felt that I should have taken an examination and joined them, rather than continue with my bare-living private business and youthful hopes of a "pie-in-the-sky" naturalist job.

My first break

My ambition to become the first salaried park naturalist, even if only for part time, resulted in several interviews with Park Superintendent Lee Kerfoot and the park commission. These worthy gentlemen made it abundantly clear that they just could not spend tax money for any such purpose. And there wasn't any Mayor Mott or Davie to appeal to.

A breakthrough came from a completely unforeseen source. A group of local business and professional men had formed what they called "The Lake Merritt Breakfast Club." They got up very early once each week to attend their breakfast session in a hotel overlooking the lake. They proclaimed themselves "Lake Merritt

11

Park Naturalist introduces migrant pintail ducks to public at 3:30 afternoon feeding.

Boosters." One eventful day in 1934, they invited me to speak to them and show them some waterfowl I had sketched.

They were convinced that I should speak for the birds and on the birds, and act as guide and greeter at the Duck Feeding Station in Lakeside Park. They offered to pay me a modest fee for my services on Sunday afternoons during the fall-winter season. They would, of course, have to clear this arrangement with the Oakland Park Commission.

I had my foot in the door—or rather an official invitation to stand inside the bird enclosure with my cardboard megaphone and preach birds and conservation. Like the starving, oil-soaked ducks of 1915, I had won official recognition. Oh, it was still a long step toward becoming a salaried park naturalist, but they would have a tough time dislodging me, I concluded.

Bugs Cain was almost as jubilant as I when he heard the news. I always suspected he may have pulled the strings that landed me this big chance. Bugs was well known to the Breakfast Club members, having got himself bitten by his pet rattlesnake while giving a reptile demonstration for the club one morning!

A part-time job as attendant and general assistant at the old Oakland Public Museum was the next bonanza to come my way. This treasure house of early California and natural history had been converted from an early mansion into a museum during Mayor Mott's regime. His sister, Susie, a dear dedicated lady, administered her lifetime responsibility as curator with gracious pride and utter devotion.

Some of the Lake Merritt birds grazed on the spacious lawns around the museum which almost touched the shores of the lake. Common egrets and black-crowned night herons roosted in the blue gum *eucalypti* that towered over the building. I was always close to the birds and, of course, took off every Sunday in the busy season to take my stand at the Refuge as "guest lecturer." The park commission had, by this time, declared me also a "volunteer park naturalist" and even requested my advice and assistance on many matters pertaining to the waterfowl maintenance operation.

World War II brought compulsory separation from my naturalist career and from the comfortable job at the museum. It eventually brought the annual duck-banding to a halt for lack of manpower, although Mr. Ehman assiduously kept up his records of distant recoveries.

The war brought other crises to the Lake and to the birds. "The wild ducks will no longer be fed at Lake Merritt due to a necessary wartime retrenchment policy," read the article that appeared in the newspapers. However, the swans and other pinioned birds given to the city for display would continue to receive regular meals.

A barrage of verbal bombshells was launched at city hall, both directly and by way of the letters-to-the-Editor columns of the daily papers. It was obvious that a war-weary Oakland still cherished the wild ducks and wasn't about to see them suffer for the sake of a small saving to the city budget.

The very pragmatic, politically-oriented official who gave the original order and press release, presumably with park commission approval, speedily reversed the decision. A newspaper editorial complimented city hall on their enlightened review of the duck feeding policy. All the waterfowl residents of Lake Merritt would go back on their once-a-day dinners!

William Penn Mott, Jr., the innovator

Something like a political A-Bomb, William Penn Mott, Jr., exploded on the Oakland scene right after World War II. Although not related to Oakland's early mayor, Bill Mott was to rock city hall, the Park and Recreation Departments, and leave his imprint on the city in a way perhaps somewhat suggestive of the impact Mayor Frank Mott had made. Bill Mott was a bright young land-scape architect with some National Park experience who promised to develop the municipal park system and give the taxpayers some new services. How he did it!

Park Superintendent Mott invited me to his office early in 1947. The Breakfast Club had also contacted me about resuming Sunday lectures at the lake, but Mott offered far more alluring opportunities. He actually wanted a full time ranger-naturalist for his park system. This he couldn't spring on the park commission and the civil service commission just like that—so, if interested, I would have to work under a park ranger classification for a few months while he, Mott, would work toward persuading the powers to establish a position of park naturalist. Bill Mott possessed supreme confidence and infectious enthusiasm. I took his offer on the spot and never regretted it.

The day I actually reported for work as a ranger-naturalist with the clear understanding that I was completely independent of the patrol ranger force, I felt something like the young minister set down in virgin territory and told to organize his flock and build a church. There was no prescribed uniform for a municipal ranger-naturalist, no office or visitor center ready to take over, and not even an official vehicle to call my own.

The ingenuity and persuasion of Superintendent Mott, the generosity and understanding of park staff friends, and the starry-visions of a nature man with a mission worked wonders. Part of the Lakeside Field Office and locker room was cleared for the new naturalist; several park supervisors and even the rival Recreation Department took turns providing me with transportation, and the Oakland Public Museum offered their lecture room for winter season indoor programs.

14

Lake Merritt and the birds remained the focal point of the new Oakland Park Naturalist Program, but there were many other opportunities and demands for the new, free naturalist's services. There were children and grownups who needed introductions to trees and birds in several outlying city parks. There were miles of unspoiled trails through chaparral and under redwoods in the hill parks. There were boys and girls catching insects, spiders, amphibians, and reptiles, or picking up things their parents and teachers couldn't identify, so they began bringing them to the ranger-naturalist. Pretty soon the tiny office was overflowing with specimens, live and otherwise.

City children watch wild animal introductions under majestic coast redwoods on Oakland's skyline.

Day camping became a craze soon after World War II. You could have it co-ed, boys or girls exclusive, all faiths, or in various denominations. The towering redwoods and pines of the Oakland skyline during several summer vacation periods played host to teeming day camps filled with children from all sections of the city.

Daily routine, ritual, games, and discipline might run a wide gamut among these various camps, but they all had one demand in common: "What day can we get the park naturalist? Our counselors can't answer half the questions the kids are asking about nature. Can he bring his snakes and lizards? Some of the new kids think the woods are full of rattlesnakes!" Et cetera, et cetera.

So the naturalist loaded up whatever vehicle he could borrow with whatever small animals he happened to have and made the day camp rounds. I might cover four to six camps and be gone all day. It was like the circus sawdust trail—only in the woods and playgrounds. I might get back to Lakeside after all the other park employees had gone home.

And there were the Girl Scouts and Brownies—and the Campfire Girls and Bluebirds—not to mention hordes of Cub Scouts. All these groups and troops of lively, insatiably curious youngsters wanted to go somewhere with "The Ranger." It was necessary to

Rosebud Skunk makes friends at summer day camp show.

16

remind them that a naturalist is a somewhat different breed of cat from a ranger. This not meant as an aspersion on rangers. They take a lot of guff and many risks that park naturalists are not so grieviously burdened with.

When the park naturalist wasn't busy with the camps and these other various groups, there were school class trips to Lake Merritt and other parks, presentations to classrooms and assemblies, and the omnipresent "general public" to entertain. Forty hour weeks didn't have much meaning for me in those days. My working examples were guys like Bill Mott and Bugs Cain who never had worried about the lengths of their working days and weeks.

What will Mott do next?

After a few months of actual services to the community, getting approval from the city council, the civil service commission, and park commission for a full time park naturalist position was no problem. A few dour taxpayers were heard to grumble, "What? A naturalist job for us to support along with all his other costly wild plans! What will that man Mott come up with next?"

Where was the new official park naturalist to be located? The Field Office-rest room building (between the "Ladies" and the "Men") continued to be the lowly nature den and office. Superintendent Mott was not happy with this arrangement and that was tantamount to change. None of us foresaw the tragic events which were to contribute toward the new home for the naturalist program.

Camp Dimond was sold by the Boy Scouts to become a public school site. The famous "Bug House" with its bird feeding and bird banding station all went down the drain of progress. Bugs Cain was shifted to other duties, but he couldn't adjust to such a drastic change. He died very suddenly in 1950. The Bug House collection and library was presented to the Oakland Park Department by his widow.

Where would this valuable collection be housed and displayed? Bill Mott was already at work on a plan. A B.C. Cain Memorial Committee was organized to raise money among Bugs' friends and admirers toward a memorial nature center. When these funds fell far short, Bill enlisted the Oakland Rotary Club to adopt the project. Then he persuaded the city council to promise to make up the remaining deficit. A friendly contractor offered to build the projected structure at what we have always suspected was a cost-*loss,* instead of a cost-plus, basis! The Rotary Natural Science Center was soon under construction, right next to the Duck Feeding Area in Lakeside Park. By September, 1953, the Oakland Park Naturalist Program had a suitable home.

Just what do you put in a brand new, empty nature center? That is—outside of the eighty-five folding chairs provided for audiences, and the office, and the B.C. Cain Memorial Nature Library.

The waterfowl of Lake Merritt, by virtue of their preeminent domain, got top billing on the high shelves of the auditorium-main exhibit room. Next, there were the live snakes which had languished in wood-wire cases those many months. Two wall panel cases were altered to accommodate these reptiles—one for the rattlesnakes and another for the harmless species. This meant the installation of small heaters, a second pane of plate glass, eighteen inches high, to restrict these pets when the large window-door was opened, and stainless steel floor trays to hold gravel bedding and water dishes.

Open your nature show with snakes and give them top billing in your animal exhibit room, brother and sister naturalists, if you would pack in audiences—not just once but for return engagements too! And if you permit Johnny or Susie to handle a harmless snake under proper supervision, they are sure to return with friends, or Mom and Dad, to show off their superior knowledge and bravery. After that you can lead them to other exhibits—perhaps even indoctrinate them subtly with some ecological understandings.

Teaching ecology with bees

Bees-in-the-wall were the next live exhibit provided for visitors to the Rotary Natural Science Center. Since then the exhibition beehive has never lacked rapt attention. Our bee watchers become even more absorbed and excited when they notice these industrious insects leaving the building and returning through small holes in the outside wall. Visitors are discouraged from intercepting the bees at their outside doorways but instead are invited to sniff honey and listen to "bee talk" through a finely screened opening on the inside.

If snakes do have an irresistible attraction for people, even for a few who hastily change seats or leave the building, I must admit that more ecology can be taught by bees. Your audience can become suddenly involved when told they would soon be without

Where the action is: Lakeside Park Duck Feeding Area, Geodesic Flight Cage, Junior Zoo, and Rotary Natural Science Center (left foreground).

many of their basic or favorite foods if men and their insecticides should also manage to wipe out their principal insect servants— the honey bees.

It was important that the Center office be placed where all visitors could find it, and they surely have ever since. Thanks to its position overlooking the park driveway, the busy Duck Feeding Area, the Junior Zoo, and the bird loafing beach and waters extending to the nearest Duck Island, it serves as both watchtower and command post. A handy public address system enables the naturalists to quickly reach any group that arrives from a school or tour bus. They are given an official greeting and a brief explanation of what goes on at that particular day and season at America's oldest wildlife refuge.

Many of the public take the naturalists' office as a sort of Grand Central information booth and the naturalist for an all-round answer man whenever he appears.

Just as the snakes and the bees "hook" the casual visitor, who then notices or studies less thrilling displays, so the live waterfowl, lined up for handouts, stop the outside passersby even if they didn't come to the park to feed birds. We estimate some half-million persons each year pass by or stop at the Duck Feeding Area in Lakeside Park. The naturalist is there too, to hand out bits of interesting information, which may include a critical conservation issue or some suggestions on behavior around wild birds and animals.

A Junior Zoo housing small native animals gradually developed around the Duck Pond. Attractive, neatly maintained cages contain skunks, raccoons, opossums, rabbits, squirrels, crows, ravens, owls, hawks, and vultures. A geodesic Dome Flight Cage, built of aluminum frame and steel mesh after the radical design introduced by Buckminster Fuller, houses rare native waterfowl, upland game birds, herons, even native jays and sparrow hawks which are compatible with the other birds. Most of these birds and mammals were rescued and hand-reared orphans, or cripples which could not have survived in the wild. These live animals enable the naturalists to present graphic lessons on conservation and to prepare city folks for occasional encounters with live animals elsewhere.

And so by these means and devices we have made our refuge, which by acreage standards is small, a place of real significance among conservation education centers of California and the United States.

Naturalist to the Rescue

*A*ny nature enthusiast who joins an urban Park Naturalist staff with the notion of spending the rest of his life interpreting nature, leading nature walks, and observing and recording natural phenomena is in for a rude awakening. Just as the average city policeman spends as little as ten percent of his time in actual crime-fighting, a metropolitan park naturalist may spend as little as twenty-five percent of his workday with lectures and guided walks. How is the rest of the time spent?

"Please help us! We've just got to have a certain bird for our play that opens next week. It calls for a seagull."

"I know this is a strange request, but my son has this pet toad, and it started to lay eggs. We've looked all over for a male toad, until someone said that you people might have one. . . ."

"Hello. This is the municipal power house, and we've got a real hangup here. One of those damn park squirrels got into the switchboard. He's chewing on the insulation and stuff and . . . what? He ain't one of yours, and why don't I call the pound? Well, for your information I did, and they're too busy chasing dogs, and besides, they haven't got the right kind of equipment . . ."

"Can you look at our pet iguana, please? It seems to have scabs and skin peeling off, and . . . what? Yes, we did take it to the vet, and he says he can't do any more for it. Please, if you'd only look at it, we might even be willing to leave it with you!"

Yes, the park naturalist gradually becomes a lending agent, counselor to lovelorn animals (and their disturbed owners), animal trouble-shooter, veterinarian surrogate, and a few other roles that were never included in the official job description. Willing or not, a naturalist subs for the local pound, the police department, and the public library. If he is lucky enough to enjoy the luxury of a clerk or telephone-answering service, he may manage to evade some of the more difficult or unreasonable requests. However, he soon finds the great range of tasks broadens his education and experience and provides a necessary service to the community.

"Please, Mister Naturalist, could you get us a dead sea gull? . . . No, we don't want it stuffed or mounted. The museum has loaned us a nice mounted gull, but our script calls for a dead-looking, rumpled gull . . . No, we can't use an old rag or bunch of chicken feathers! We must have a real gull!"

The voice was male, agitated, and tremulous. He identified himself as the director of a San Francisco theatre company; his play would open next week. Time was running out, but he knew we could help them.

I explained with equal insistence that all gulls were protected by law. We just couldn't go out and shoot one, script or no script. However, we might be able to pick up a gull carcass and fix it up. They could apply for a permit to keep it for a prop, or we might consider it a loan.

I started the search for a dead gull along the Lake Merritt shores, but it seemed all the gulls, hundreds of them, were remarkably healthy that week. I couldn't find even an old carcass. Finally, we had to give the director the bad news.

The director, the cast, and stagehands must then have embarked on an all-out canvass of the bay shores and garbage dumps, for one of them delivered a very dead gull to us on the following day. Fortunately, one of the volunteer naturalist aides was able to scrape off the maggots and prepare quite a presentable "dead gull" specimen. It was finished just in time for opening night.

The director sent two complimentary tickets, but we never got around to seeing "our" bird on stage.

Rescuing stranded ducks and geese

Crises of vanishing duck habitats frequently make news. Prairie potholes, marsh ponds, and sloughs drained and usurped by agriculture are all too familiar to sportsmen and waterfowl management people, but for urban duck lovers, this sort of crisis is quite novel and they are usually unprepared. And so it happened in May 1964 to the stranded ducks and geese of Cascade Lake in Orinda.

Cascade Lake fills with winter rains and even attracts a few interesting wild ducks. It also serves as a collection center and sanctuary for a colony of white Pekin ducks—the Easter ducklings which must be "dumped" somewhere as they grow fat, noisy, and less cherished. (The "duck dumping" problem is well known at public park ponds across the country, where periodic roundups are necessary to reduce the domestic duck population before they imperil the municipal feeding budget and crowd all desirable wild ducks from the premises.) The sympathetic Orinda home-owners, unwilling to exercise control over their treasured duck pond, except to throw in bits of food, phoned the authorities when the inevitable crisis arose.

The Oakland Park naturalist staff was perhaps the sixth agency to receive their appeal for help. They urgently requested we send a rescue expedition to round up the Pekins, a domestic goose, and a solitary Canada goose which had also joined the party. It was difficult to refuse these desperate ladies. They had already been turned down by their Contra Costa County Pound, the Oakland City Pound, the S.P.C.A., and the local Fish and Game Warden. I warned them that if they hired local men to round them up, these tame ducks could be left at Lake Merritt with the understanding that they would later be sent to some charitable institution for duck dinners.

Needless to say, this suggestion was not well received. At this point an extremely sympathetic member of the naturalist staff volunteered to go out on his own time to attempt the rescue operation. Judging from ensuing telephone conversations, it qualified him as an on-the-spot Orinda hero.

The expedition that left for Cascade Lake the next afternoon was a formidable one. Paraphernalia included rubber hip boots, catching nets of two sizes, boxes, and gunny sacks. One wife and one very capable teenage son had joined the rescue party by this time, and the mission was further buoyed by the assurance that, once caught, the pound would take them to hold for adoption.

Darkness set in early. The mud was deep under the shallow water. And the quarry proved to be more alert and elusive than size or shape would indicate. But all twenty fat Pekins were finally rounded up and sacked. The tame goose had disappeared, and the Canada goose—the one bird that would have been welcomed at Lake Merritt—had simply flown off, in search of its own kinfolk no doubt.

Then came the bombshell finale: no pound or other shelter would take the birds. They were placed in a little outlying park pond which was already overcrowded with such domestics. Here, sadly, the fate of being caught for an institutional mess hall still awaited them. What, we wondered, would the good ladies of Orinda say to that?

Ladies in distress

A call one day from a woman about a stray duck didn't appear to be extraordinary or fraught with explosive emotional accompaniments. She called merely to inform us that "a white duck with a red face" had suddenly materialized in her garden, that she didn't want it, and could she please bring it to Lake Merritt. We said she could.

The big, white muscovy duck arrived at the Duck Pond in short order and was set down in the surrounding yard to run free. There was a drake named Bareface present—one of the typical uncouth, underwashed, leering, and lascivious males which found his own mate quite insufficient for his amorous designs. Soon Bareface was pursuing the new muscovy maiden round and round the area, and it appeared that she might at any moment tire from the chase and join his harem.

Later the same afternoon, there was a frantic phone call from a man who had just learned that his Genevieve (a white muscovy duck) had been picked up by a neighbor and delivered to us. If it

24

were true, he wanted to know, could he get her back — and right away, before something happened to her? We said yes if he would come down and identify her. And that he did with stunning promptness.

When the gentleman arrived, it was almost time for the daily feeding and lecture. Immediately, he spotted Genevieve in a group of other ducks. He called to her, first in English and then in his native Italian. As Genevieve bobbed her head in typical muscovy fashion, hissed toward her owner, and made no move to give herself up, the gentleman became more and more agitated. To avert a headlong chase around the yard and complete disruption of my daily talk, I promised to send the birdkeeper in with a net to

capture Genevieve right after the feeding tour. This plan pacified him somewhat, but it was obvious that he was very upset.

Twenty minutes later Genevieve was recaptured without too much resistance. The gentleman approached me, errant duck in his arms and tears in his eyes. His voluble gratitude and unconcealed emotion reached everyone standing nearby. He would have given anything to get her back, he told us. She laid him an egg nearly every morning, he added. I suppose it was bad taste for me to ask if that was why he valued her so dearly!

One spring a mallard brood hatched in a sunken plant box two stories above street level at the county courthouse. The young could not make the eighteen-inch upward jump to the granite rim of the box for the leap to the street. Office girls on the three floors above were watching this dilemma from windows, wringing their hands in anxious wonder, and neglecting county business. The gardener working across the street had declined to help, pleading acrophobia.

An SOS from the courthouse appealed to the "Duck Man" to rescue the family. I hastily gathered a net, a box, and some grain as bait and took off. A courthouse window cleaner accompanied me when I reached the scene. We were forced to walk a narrow ledge with all the rescue equipment to reach the corner "bird" box. The hen remained with her family until we made one pass with the net. Then she managed to escape and fly a short distance away to an inaccessible ledge. I was able to gather the nine ducklings, but had no choice but to leave not only the hen (complaining from the opposite ledge), but also an indeterminate number of sympathetic human "hens" (grieving loudly from windows above).

After a short jaunt across the street to inspect the gardener's new planting, I returned to my station wagon to find the courthouse girls still watching the mother. They pleaded with me to save the hen, so there I was back on the ledge, with only a single duckling for company. I released the duckling, lured the mother very close, but could not get the net on her. Finally, I had to leave, unsure whether I had become a hero or a villain in the eyes of the courthouse girls. However, I did find a good foster mother for the ducklings at the Duck Pond, and that was more important.

A young collector brought in a placid native toad for the spring terrarium. One day it startled us by grinding out long strings of gelatin-like egg casing. We might have been satisfied to use them as a temporary weekend display, with no thoughts of hatching more toads, but not the junior volunteer aides.

"We've got to find a male to fertilize them before it's too late," they announced.

Jim remembered that a friend kept some toads at home and might have a male. Because these creatures are rather modest about displaying their sex, it would be necessary to introduce as many toads as possible, on the chance that one would be interested. Jim was authorized to use the office phone to call his friend. The ensuing conversation might have startled any operator listening in. It seemed the toad owner had to present a very convincing argument before his parents would drive him to the Science Center.

Apparently the argument was persuasive, for within the half hour the youngster appeared proudly bearing two fat complacent toads who seemed little aware of their crucial roles. They were immediately introduced into the same tank as the determined egg-layer, who by this time was almost totally enveloped by her own mass production. But the newcomers failed to become excited by the situation and declined to prove themselves, either by discharging their masculine duties or by joining in the egg-laying marathon.

Wild animals at City Hall

One fall day, an insistent call from the electrician at Oakland City Hall summoned us to come quickly and remove a fox squirrel from the power control room or prescribe and provide some means of trapping the animal. Nobody could figure out how it got there, but it was scampering over the master switches, sampling the flavor of various knobs and insulated cables, and creating considerable apprehension in general.

Since I didn't relish the prospect of dashing among the switches with a steel frame net, I suggested shooting the animal with a .410, only to learn that it hid from sight most of the day. Then I suggested setting a live trap, but it developed that the squirrel had possibly escaped into the basement. So it was decided to hold off a day with the trap.

The next day a photographer at the city hall press room phoned. Could I come down immediately? The squirrel had been trapped in a carton outside in the big light well adjacent to the power room. It would make a good newsreel story when we captured the squirrel and then released it in the park. However, it might not remain too long in the carton, so hurry.

I scurried off equipped with a photogenic aluminum animal transfer case, a pair of heavy gloves, a net, and even a live trap in the event the squirrel escaped us completely. I met the news photographer and another reporter at the press room. By the time we were escorted through a window into the light well and the photographer had posted his camera at the sidewalk level, we realized we had accumulated quite a gallery of spectators.

I threw open the door of the aluminum case (into which I planned to drop the squirrel from the carton) and what should trot out of the case but a possum! A quick guess was that the animalkeeper on duty the preceding day had picked up a stray possum, put it into the case, and absentmindedly forgot to take it out.

27

Well, we safely transferred the squirrel to the carrying case, while the half-grown possum ran around the light well to amuse the crowd and give the photographer some extra shots. Then we rushed both squirrel and possum back to Lakeside Park, where the camera man took more footage on the happy squirrel as it scampered across the lawn toward the nearest oak tree. It all came out pretty well on the evening news, except for the embarrassing possum that mysteriously popped out of the aluminum case.

Providing mates for the lovelorn

Nature conflicts, like human history, repeat and repeat. Yet each incident involving Man vs. Bird is so real and gripping to the principals involved that it may seem like the very first in human history.

For instance, a senior citizen couple impatiently awaited my arrival one day in the Center lobby. The birdkeeper on duty had listened to their story for as long as he could and then turned them over to me.

The wife did not hesitate to describe their problem, and as she told it, became so emotionally disturbed, I feared she was going to break down and weep. Her husband stood by for moral support, but it was obvious he shared his wife's feelings. Their problem was not a new one.

Last spring they had innocently adopted a tiny, cuddly duckling, not caring what kind it was. Since they owned a suburban home with an acre of land, they knew Greenie would have plenty of room to roam as it grew.

And grow Greenie did. Soon after, it acquired a juvenile green-tinged plumage, strong evidence that it was a drake. A few weeks later it became a handsome full-grown drake specimen, but still completely attached to its human foster parents. *Imprinted* is the term animal behaviorists use for birds and animals reared by people and thus come to regard themselves as "people."

In the bird biological process, Greenie quite naturally developed the proper male glands and began looking for a mate. As there was no understanding female mallard in sight, he followed the only course he knew. When the man of the house came out to feed or talk to him, he seized the cuff of his pants and tried to mount his shoe!

After a few weeks, the poor gentleman had several frayed pants cuffs, and even worse, two chewed-upon ankles. He lifted his trousers to exhibit them, and then his wife showed me the bruises on her lower legs. Even her hands and wrists were bruised, her reward for trying to pet and soothe the drake.

But getting rid of their dear Greenie had been simply unthinkable, so they took their problem to a local veterinarian. Could he operate perhaps, as with a dog or a cat? Well, maybe, but he'd rather not. Instead, he suggested they take Greenie to his friend, Dr. Young, director of the Knowland Zoo.

The ingenious Dr. Young handled the problem with customary dispatch. He sent the "parents" of the lovelorn duck to Lake Merritt. "See Paul Covel. He'll know what to do."

Well, this was a familiar problem in our bird vs. people counseling affairs. "How would you like to borrow a mate for Greenie?" we asked.

They immediately agreed. How soon could they get one? And what would stop her from flying away if she didn't accept this blind-date marriage?

"You will have to come back for the hen," we explained. She couldn't be just any attractive mallard around the Duck Pond. The bride would have to be an oversize, unmistakable hybrid type, thanks to the recent rulings of the Fish and Wildlife Service which decreed that all "free-flying mallard-type ducks" were under game law protection.

A few days later we captured a large, lumbering hybrid hen. To be certain she couldn't fly away from her suitor, we clipped a few feathers on one wing. Then we phoned the couple. Within the hour the gentleman arrived carrying a small carton designed for bird transportation. He winced a bit when we brought in Monstrous Myrtle, but eased her bulk into the carrying case anyway.

"Do you think our Greenie will accept her?" he asked dubiously.

"Oh sure, any duck's a mate to a lovelorn drake," we assured him. "Just in case they don't hit it off, bring her back and we'll try another.

We never did get a report from the scene of action so we assumed the mating was happily consummated.

Adventures with Wild Pets

As an indulgent parent, have you ever been confronted with questions, tearful pleas, or agonizing decisions like the following:

"Look, Mom, what we just found on the sidewalk—four baby birds with their eyes still closed. We can't find their nest or their parents anywhere! Can't we feed them, please?"

"It's a squirrel, Dad! We found it in the road; it's not hurt too bad—it just has a broken leg. Can we fix it and keep it Dad? Please."

"Hey, guess what! The pet shop has a darling baby fox in the window. And it's cheap! Oh, I've got to have it. It'll make a great pal for Skip."

As a naturalist who has observed people-pet reactions, I feel that a defense of pet-keeping by urban and suburban youth is in order. I don't want to see future naturalists frustrated in their formative years. In my earliest years, as a city-born, city-apartment, and city-park captive, I was never allowed pets except during short summer vacations in the countryside outside Boston. Wild pets captured on those summer adventures were limited to small creatures like turtles, frogs, toads, or insects.

My first big break happened at Wellesley, Massachusetts, where we rented a cottage for an entire season. The landlord was a former entomological collector for a Massachusetts college museum, and he actually helped me set up a tank for tadpoles and another for frogs, toads, and salamanders. His name is long forgotten, but his encouragement and understanding of an eight-year-old nature boy created one of the brightest chapters in my childhood. A horrible skin eruption caused by the hairs of the prevalent gypsy moths and equally painful bouts with poison ivy were traumatic experiences for my parents, but for me they were only normal risks incurred in getting close to nature.

Two years later I was really liberated from city living when my parents purchased a year-round home at South Weymouth, close to pasture, woods, and swampland. An understanding neighbor introduced me to the use of shotguns, .22 rifles, and traps. I became a private control agent for woodchucks and crows, paid per scalp by neighborhood farmers, but my fur-trapping success was limited mainly to skunks which netted me meager profits but had fringe benefits of keeping me home from school on several occasions.

Yet my instinctive preference for wild animal keeping and study often submerged my hunting and trapping activities. That is how our backyard became tenanted with woodchucks and cottontail rabbits which had either escaped or been set free after brief sojourns as pets. This situation my former friends and patrons frowned on, and my long-suffering parents were shaken still further by the neighbor's hounds' nightly hunts staged in our backyard.

We returned to city life when we moved to San Diego, California. As a teenager, I immediately discovered and made friends at the popular zoo and at the natural history museum. After I acquired a car, together with buddies Sam and Jack, endowed with similar interests and enthusiasm, we combed Southern California from seacoast to mountains to desert to collect and study the flora and fauna. We were particularly fortunate at this time to win the confidence of a pioneer naturalist-collector, Frank Stephens, who took us along with him on local collecting expeditions and taught us valuable lessons in the natural history of the Southwest.

This is how one incipient boy naturalist "got the breaks," thanks to parents who yielded to his pleas that city life was destroying him. The average urban youngster does not ordinarily get such opportunities. However, thanks to modern school programs, community field trips, urban nature centers, in-school camps or sponsored summer camp experiences, educational TV and films in the Disney tradition, children with latent nature curiosity do get some exposure to wild pets.

But there is no real substitute for actual possession of a pet by a youngster. In these times of racial tension, economic stress, and other frustrations of urban living, the companionship and responsibility of a live pet exerts an enriching experience on its youthful owner. If the pet can't be a cat or a dog, it may have to be a budgie, canary, pigeon, or even a lowly turtle. A wild animal pet may never be available to many children, but for those fortunate households which do acquire wild pets, let's consider some of the effects of captivity on the animals themselves. There are a few prevalent illusions and misconceptions which should be exposed to the light of fact and truth.

Animals are not people

Many animal "humanizers" convince themselves that animals suffer from pain and loneliness as keenly as do humans. This belief causes needless concern or even conflict which may involve the persons in charge of modern, well-housed, live animal exhibits. There is little evidence to indicate that even the most intelligent mammals, like the dog, cat, raccoon, or fox can conceive or project mental images of suffering or deprivation beyond their immediate situation, which would compare with the trauma of a human kept as a captive among strangers. I share the disgust and indignation of those who find wild animals in cramped, ill-kept cages in roadside zoos or menageries, but I am equally concerned over the propaganda campaigns of organized "zoo-haters" who would eliminate even the most modern, progressive, and invaluable zoological institution.

Wild animals captured very young or taken in as orphans and reared by humans seldom benefit by escaping or being

33

returned to the wild. In fact, they seldom survive when given freedom. Some of the episodes related in this book might be construed otherwise, but a closer reflection will show that even the park pets that "escaped" still depended on man for a living, and took care to remain under our general protection.

This is not intended to disparage the humane treatment of wild animal pets—far from it. Their living quarters should be as spacious as possible and, in the case of birds and mammals, there must be small corners of privacy provided for them. They do *not* have to be completely screened from view. A glass jar within the larger cage will quickly be adopted by most rodents as a sleeping den or retreat, and it can be capped quickly and used to transfer the pet when the cage is cleaned or moved to another location. Shatterproof glass or heavy plastic sleeping boxes permit many animal rooms to reveal their occupants, even when sleeping or resting. In a small cage, an exercise wheel is a must for members of the squirrel family and for other normally lively small mammals.

Another widespread misconception of wild pet keeping is an impassioned desire of humans to see their wild pets with mates. Most wild birds and mammals do not even live together as pairs throughout the year. Many small mammals meet only for mating and then quickly separate. If you force a constant cohabitation upon them, you may doom them to discord or actual strife which may result in your losing them. Now I like romance and blessed events among wild pets as much as any of the nature romantics. But I wonder how many of these sentimentalists who ignore the true habits of wild animals would lavish such concern upon the lonely widows, widowers, or orphan children in their communities?

As for the coatis, kinkajous, ocelots, marguey cats, and monkeys—who brought these exotic animals into the country and sold them to eager customers who wound up with vexing problems? If I answer that, I must point accusingly to many animal dealers who imported and sold any sort of beast a customer would buy. The only requirements were that the animal be young enough to handle, tough enough to survive shipment, and stay alive until someone took it home. Few pet stores guaranteed that their exotic "pets" would grow to maturity or remain tame and affectionate.

Even now, if you want a boa constrictor, caiman, or baby red fox, it is your responsibility as a wild animal keeper to read up on that species, or consult a keeper at your zoo, or a curator in the nearest museum. That bit of research could save you a lot of grief, disappointment, and wasted money.

Thousands of American nature buffs and conservationists became concerned over the impact of this mounting exotic pet

Who will win this one? A confrontation between the horned owl and a pussycat.

demand on populations of animals in their native countries. It seemed that the profits reaped by the collectors and importers would wipe out the source. Few of these exotic pets reproduce in captivity except occasionally under conditions found in modern zoos with competent staffs.

Endangered species legislation

Action was demanded. In 1969, Congress passed the Endangered Species Act which permits the government to ban the importation and interstate transportation for sale of species of birds and mammals which have been declared by competent authorities to be "endangered." Exceptions were made by the federal legislation for legitimate zoological gardens and other scientific institutions, although cumbersome bureaucratic procedures have seriously hampered efficient exchange among zoos.

With this ban on exotic mammals, the demand for reptile pets zoomed. Turtles and tortoises, lizards, snakes, and amphibians, both imported and domestic, proliferated in pet stores from coast to coast. Many of these creatures have exacting dietary needs and soon sicken and die. Federal authorities banned the trading of all turtles under four inches in width, unless they received health certificates at the point of origin. This didn't even take congressional action. The paternal and protective Department of Health, Education and Welfare decided that too many Americans were catching salmonella from pet turtles—particularly the sizes small children could fondle and kiss!

California recently enacted legislation prohibiting possession of virtually all native animals except those taken by hunters and trappers in season. Instead of this harsh, sweeping edict, one banning the traffic in native mammals by the pet trade would have been adequate. The law did include a provision for issuance of individual permits to keep orphaned or injured animals, but in so doing, it set up a costly bureaucratic operation. The youngster who adopts a squirrel, chipmunk, gopher, vole, or possum isn't likely to meddle with this procedure.

Suppose your neighbor decides to raise a lion or bear cub? When it grows too large for the house, he stakes it out in the backyard on a leash or chain. "It's as tame and affectionate as a puppy,"he calls confidently across the fence to his skeptical neighbors. Meanwhile, the beast has wrestled him to the ground and is chewing playfully on his neck. Will you be its next unwilling playmate?

It is apparent that urban yards are not suitable habitat for large wild animals. People taking that cute cub soon find that it grows into something more than they can handle and then try to give it away. All in one spring-summer season, among native mammals offered—and rejected—by unhappy citizens for the junior zoo at the Natural Science Center were a bear cub, Alaskan wolf, bobcat, two grey foxes, and numerous mature raccoons and skunks. Any city government is justified in passing ordinances prohibiting the keeping of potentially dangerous pets by private citizens. But the language of the law should read, ". . . animals which might become dangerous or nuisances in the community. . . ." or something to that effect.

At the same time, I would urge local lawmakers not to go so far as to ban all animal pets except dogs, cats, cage birds, and fish as have some American municipalities. That boy's pet possum, squirrel, or garter snake may be far less of a nuisance than one yapping dog. Many small wild animals rescued and adopted as orphans become interesting pets which stimulate entire neighborhoods and classrooms to nature awareness.

Rabies is a very real threat to those who capture skunks and foxes for pets. In fact, many states and counties have banned pet sales and trade in skunks. Raccoons, possums, and rodents appear much less susceptible to rabies, but the rabies-carrying propensity of bats is well established. If you have a baby skunk or fox, it should receive rabies shots as soon as your veterinarian will give them.

Caring for injured or ailing pets

If you, living in a metropolitan area, have a health or accident problem with your pet turtle, lizard, snake, chipmunk, budgie, canary, hamster, or rabbit, I hope you picked up one of the excellent, inexpensive handbooks on your type of pet. Unless you are fortunate enough to have an "all-animal" veterinarian (my terminology) nearby, you and your pet are in trouble. A regular veterinarian with whom you have established business relations through dog or cat treatments may give you some advice and even consent to examine your ailing pet. But the typical dog-and-cat vet may not know much more about the habits of your native animal pet than you do. Even with the cage-bird or the rabbit, a vet may feel unprepared to treat or prescribe. And did you ever run the gauntlet of those whining growling canines in the doctor's waiting room while trying to shield and comfort a frightened budgie or bunny?

What this country needs—if I may use an overworked phrase —is more veterinarians and clinics specializing in cage-birds and small pets, the kinds millions of urban and suburban dwellers have. There should be lucrative practices awaiting vets who would perform such services. I remember a charming lady vet who maintained a "house call" practice in and around our city many years ago. She might have made a modest fortune if her sympathy and generosity hadn't compelled her to donate so many hours in treating the domestic animals at Children's Fairyland and the little wild pets at the Natural Science Center.

Does your community have a major problem with the rescue and treatment of orphaned and injured wild birds and mammals? A really successful project in wild pet rescue and rearing has been carried on in recent years at the popular Alexander Lindsay Junior Museum in Walnut Creek, California. It serves as an inspiration and demonstration of what can be done by a community.

From early spring until late summer a procession of rescuers brings orphaned and injured wild animals to this facility. Small boys and girls, distraught mothers, policemen, animal shelter and S.P.C.A. drivers, state game wardens, and federal wildlife agents all head for this junior museum which is housed in a converted public utility building in a small public park. Many modern, costly children's museums or nature centers with landscaped approaches, lavish offices, and elegant visitor facilities would envy the reputation, the dedicated volunteer corps, and the impact on surrounding communities enjoyed by the Alexander Lindsay Junior Museum.

Gary Bogue, the head foundling father, a naturalist of inexhaustible patience and kindness, insists that one of the main reasons for his phenomenal success with so many wild orphans is due to a nearby veterinarian who collaborates with Gary on all medical problems of rescued animals. Together with Director Sam Smoker they have worked out successful and sometimes new methods of saving and treating delicate and difficult baby birds and mammals.

38

Imagine each day having fifteen to twenty baby birds dumped in your lap so to speak! Add to those a family of cottontail or brush rabbits, baby raccoons, a wobbly-legged bleating fawn, and a few assorted young hawks and owls. You wonder how a man with these responsibilities, plus the duties of instructing and supervising the adult and juvenile volunteers who share this load, ever finds a day or even a night off. The answer is—he doesn't. Many of the more demanding wild orphans go home with Gary each evening.

Problems with wild orphans

When I dropped in at Alexander Lindsay one day in late May, among high-priority, special patients were two young golden eagles. A game warden had brought in one from another county and the second had been left on the doorstep of a veterinarian. Evidence later indicated they had both been stolen from the same nest. One eaglet was in a fast-declining condition—"terminal" as the medics say—suffering from rickets when it got to Gary. For a few nights, he kept cranking the overworked Bogue family alarm clock to awaken hourly to tenderly stuff pieces of vitamin-loaded meat down the youngster's throat. When other duties kept Gary away for an evening, his family took over the eaglet feeding as they had done so many times previously with other animal orphans.

A new stage or breakthrough had just been reached the next week when I dropped in to check on the eagles' progress. They had actually seized, killed, and eaten live rats offered to them in the Bogues' yard. "That's great," said Gary, "but now I'll have to build them a pen at home, because they just might decide to grab our family cat."

These young golden eagles were about six weeks old on this occasion. A horned owl of about the same age shared their open pen at the museum in hopes it would imitate the actions of the eaglets who eagerly accepted and bolted down their food. Captive owl babies generally become chow hounds after one or two force feedings. This one must have been a backward child.

"What future is there for the golden eagles, assuming they grow into full eaglehood with normal physical power and perception?" I asked Gary. I knew that in a natural state they would be fed, then hunt with the mother for some months before they could make it on their own.

Gary shook his head. "I'm afraid they'll wind up as zoo specimens unless someone can show them how to hunt in the field, using released rabbits or other small animals. I may ask the U.S. Fish and Wildlife fellows if I can work with a professional falconer who would know how to give such lessons."

I asked about the initial stages of fawn care, as I knew the museum accepted three or more of these babies each year and boasted a good record in bringing them through infancy.

"We don't have too many problems if they pick up the fawns after the fifth day," explained Gary. "The vet and I figured out it takes that long for the youngsters to build up colostrum in their stomachs. Colostrum, the mother's first milk, is the natural protection against many kinds of infection. We manage to save about two fawns out of each three brought to us."

"By the way, did you see my last column in the *Times?*" he asked. Gary writes a weekly column on wild animal pets for the local paper. "I'm trying to persuade people not to buy foxes from the pet dealers. They are being dumped all over the county as they grow up and cause problems to their keepers. Trapping and selling so many local grey foxes and baby raccoons is bad enough and must have an adverse effect on the ecology of the county. Foxes and raccoons make lousy pets. They are little darlings for the first two to four months. After that, they become flighty, nervous, and may bite, snarl or hide. They're nocturnal and want to sleep all day and play noisily at night. They may literally tear your house apart from curiosity. Besides the foxes have a heavy musk in their urine and urinate as a sign of affection or interest."

A busy pet lending library has long been a popular service of the Alexander Lindsay Junior Museum—a custom shared with many junior museums and nature centers around this country. Rabbits, guinea pigs, and hamsters constitute the principal loans. Wild animal pets are not ordinarily loaned except tortoise, turtles, lizards, or snakes occasionally for educational purposes. The museum operates under the municipal recreation department, and the city attorneys dislike claims or lawsuits over wild animal pet bites.

A visit in the general animal room at this junior museum is a revelation in people versus wild pet reactions. Several mature hawks and owls stare down from perches around the walls— they're grown-up orphans or wing-cripples which could never

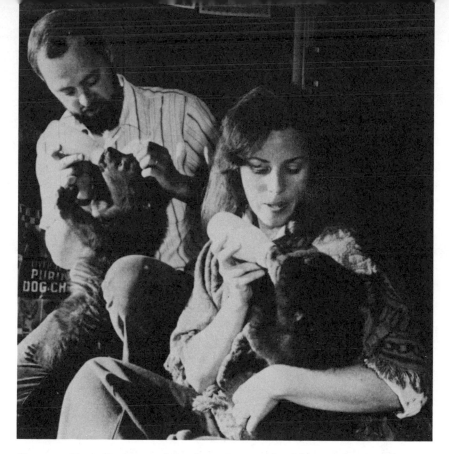

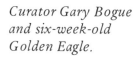

Curator Gary Bogue and Barbara Bogue feed bear cubs at Alex Lindsay Junior Museum.

Raptor Specialist Dave Garcelon and rehabilitated Bald Eagle.

Curator Gary Bogue and six-week-old Golden Eagle.

survive outdoors. Raccoons, skunks, wild rabbits, and squirrels accept proffered snacks from children's fingers with utmost gentleness and good manners. A miscellany of blackbirds, starlings, robins, shrikes, mockingbirds, and meadowlarks sharing a tall wire enclosure in mid-floor are fed by visitors who dip puppy kibbles in water and offer them on tweezers through the mesh. Truly, this is a modern Noah's Ark on a child's scale, I thought.

Care and feeding of orphaned birds

This brings us to the nitty-gritty problem of orphaned baby birds. No doubt you have gone through heart-rending experiences when a bird foundling has been brought to your doorstep, especially if you enjoy the reputation of being a bird lover in your community. Excited children rush in and place a tiny blob of flesh and pinfeathers in your hands. "Oh, we've got to save it! We can't let it die! What do we do?" they ask with implicit faith in your ability to restore the bird to health.

The chances are that your concern for the children as well as the helpless victim will overcome your judgement and convictions. I have observed, counseled, and shared in these baby bird rescues for years. I'm afraid the truth is brutal about these salvage attempts. In the first place, the odds of success are heavily stacked against you. If your orphan doesn't have a few pinfeathers, eyes open, and lusty movements, please destroy it mercifully for your chances of saving it and rearing it are really infinitesimal.

The young of songbirds, once fallen from their nests, are among the most difficult of all wild babies to feed. Their natural diet consists of small worms, spiders, and a rich variety of insects and insect larvae, with some bits of greens and fruits. Meals are served at frequent intervals from dawn to sundown by devoted parents. They may even be predigested, regurgitated, and pumped into junior's gullet. If you are reaching for bread and milk, forget it. And you won't need an eye-dropper unless you have a baby hummingbird or to give your patient a *few drops of water* each day.

For baby's food, use puppy kibbles and some softbilled bird food. If you wish to prepare your own formula, here are ingredients recommended by Mrs. William Voss of Oakland, an expert on care of baby birds: a mixture of bits of raw ground liver or other lean meat, a small quantity of mashed or grated fruits and wild green tops, hard boiled egg moistened with a little orange juice, thin milk, or water. If you feed the puppy kibbles, so successfully used at the Alexander Lindsay Junior Museum, be sure they are soaked to a soft consistency before feeding. Wheat germ may be added sparingly to any of the above food mixtures.

You present this tasty goulash gently to your bird baby at the end of a small forceps, smooth stick, glass tube, or even using your own little finger. The little rascal then clams up and refuses to open its bill. He'll starve first, the miserable waif, before he'll open up for this monster. This is just your first rebuff. Don't give up.

Obviously, a different approach is called for. You might try tapping gently on, above, or below the bill. It might work, but the chances are you are going to have to pry the beak open, using a blunt instrument. A seven-inch long orange stick with flat, blunt ends is good for this purpose. Once you pry that little bill open, you must hold it while you stuff down a few small portions of food, and perhaps massage a bit to get it swallowed. Then, and only then, may baby get the idea and eagerly open wide each time you approach with food.

If your bird-baby decides to eat regularly, that means hourly meals from dawn to dusk! If your other responsibilities do not permit you to take on this routine, you'll have to look for a bird-sitter. Did you ever try telling the boss you had to stay home with a baby bird? Or send word to the school office that junior had to stay home for such a purpose? It might be better just to take the baby, formula, and all along to office or school. Think of the entertainment and nature education you will provide. More than once I've watched a bird-sitter take time out during a meeting to feed a bird baby.

If a baby mourning dove—or even a small squab of the domestic pigeon—has landed in your care, still different formulas and methods are demanded. If very small, start off with hard-boiled egg yolk moistened well with cream or whole milk. As it grows and moves out of the nest, add the chopped greens, wheat germ, and even some ground oats. Doves and pigeons can drink like man and mammals without tipping up the head to swallow like most other birds. But the young will not ordinarily reach for food like the others. You will need both hands to force open their beaks and to place their food inside until they are grown.

If baby bob white or other quail, grouse, pheasant, ducklings, or goslings should become your charges, your feeding chores will be much lighter. These precocious babies pick up their own food like baby chicks under parental guidance. Get the proper mash, scatter before the babes and peck a bit with a finger or pencil and they usually get the idea. The mash must be moistened for ducklings and goslings.

Any box lined with paper towels or rags isn't exactly the ideal home for your bird child, but it may serve for awhile. However, you must keep it clean. You can fashion an imitation nest from dry grass or straw where the baby can flex its feet and stretch up into the light. This will aid its sanitary discharges and help tone all its muscles. When the youngster begins to pick up its own food, have some gravel handy for that important food-grinding in the stomach.

Now, what do I do?

Now, are you prepared to teach a fledgling bird to fly? We're assuming the little stinker did actually make it this far. Watch for its little flight feathers to unfold. Get the bird on your finger or on a pencil on the edge of the "nest" or box, and bounce gently to force using the wings for balance. Then pick the day and the time when the trainee is ready to solo down to the table or floor. Note: it shouldn't be necessary for you to flap your arms and make like a bird to bring this about.

If you are lucky enough to progress this far with a baby bird, it is now time to plan "Graduation Day." If you're really lucky, the parent birds may still be around the neighborhood with fledged babies, and you can release your charge nearby, hoping it will join its natural kin. But remember, it hasn't been briefed on cats and other dangers of the outside world, and may not last out the hour. The sad facts are that you may have to keep your rescued fledgling forever. The bird has become imprinted on you, as the animal behaviorists say, and is completely unfit for a natural life. Now what? Do you build a cage and get into the aviculture fraternity?

You see, I should have been more brutal and factual and never let you get this far. You are not only in deep trouble with the children, the landlord, and your budget, but you are a law violator. That's right, unless you rescued a so-called "blacklisted species," like house sparrows and starlings, you are violating the federal Migratory Bird Treaty and perhaps one or two of your state game laws.

The scientists, law enforcement officials, government representatives, and legal advisors who framed this generally admirable set of laws in the 1920's and 1930's just didn't or couldn't figure out what to do about rescuers and keepers of protected orphaned birds. Every day you keep that bird baby, you are guilty of a federal violation. However, most of the state fish and game or conservation departments are empowered to issue individual permits allowing you to possess a protected bird if you can demonstrate that it is not capable of being released in the wild. So, if you must keep that bird, you had better waste no time in contacting your nearest game warden or other conservation officer.

You may ask how come our state and federal penitentiaries aren't full of good samaritan bird rescuers. It happens that most of these bird adoptions are just never reported to the forces of law. Also, when they do come to the attention of local authorities, the average officer is sympathetic and reluctant to crack down on the foster bird home.

Shouldn't municipal zoos, natural history museums, pounds, or S.P.C.A. shelters be expected or even required to take in these foundling birds and mammals? Should the nearest veterinarian be expected to treat them free of charge or at a nominal rate? That might be desirable and ethical, but it doesn't work that way. Staffs and personnel of most of these institutions are too busy with other duties to assume the care of such unfortunates. For merely calling for your bird or mammal orphan or cripple, the local pound or S.P.C.A. may charge a pickup fee, as for a cat or dog— if, indeed, they will even answer your request!

So what is the answer for all the good people who find they just have to be wildlife rescuers? If there isn't a nature center like Alexander Lindsay nearby, you might get together with a sympathetic vet, your local Audubon group, some dedicated citizens, or your area game protectors and set up a recognized foundation for such services. Token support from city or county lends official status and takes a load off other public agencies and officers.

Wildfowl I Could Live with: Canada Geese, *Their Kin, and a Loner*

*I*f the United States should ever allow progress and pesticides to exterminate our national bird, the American or Bald Eagle, I have a number one candidate for this symbol and this honor. I am pretty sure my candidate will be around long after the last eagle is mourned and placed in a museum.

The Canada goose accepts man, his man-made habitats, and his protection. It is the only North American native goose that willingly remains and nests in the contiguous States while all other migrant geese return to the far north each spring. Of course, thousands of Canadas also return north across Canada to nest in cooler summer climes, and these migrants attract far more attention than the ones that remain to nest in the Great Basin and Pacific Northwest.

Canada geese of the Atlantic Flyway passing over Lake Erie found a friend and protector in Jack Miner at Kingsville, Ontario, whose farm eventually became world famous as the Jack Miner Migratory Bird Foundation. This race known as the Atlantic Canada Goose has been established in the British Isles, Iceland,

and New Zealand. In this last country, Canada geese have multiplied to well over twenty thousand, threaten the crops, and are bagged at all seasons!

In the days of Indian occupation and of the grizzlies and elk herds, Canada geese no doubt stopped off to rest and feed on the marshes that stretched inland from the present location of Lake Merritt. But they ceased to visit when the marshes were filled, and homes and park lands enclosed the remaining lake. While wild ducks and many other waterfowl continued to flock in, the wily Canadas or honkers stayed away, though they did come as close as the reservoirs across the hills in Contra Costa County, and still winter on and around these waters.

Wild geese return to Oakland

Occasionally some pen-reared or crippled Canadas were brought and released on Lake Merritt, and less frequently, two of these birds would mate and nest on the Old Duck Island, but they received little protection. As soon as I moved in as a full-time park naturalist, I determined to build up a flock of these desirable birds, and to bring in any other native geese we could get. Appeals were sent to refuge managers, ranchers, and goose hunters in the Sacramento Valley.

I'll never forget that trip to a farm near Dixon in the Sacramento Valley one rainy spring day. A farmer had invited me to take several of the wing-crippled Canadas he had accumulated over several hunting seasons. He wanted to keep only a couple of nesting pairs, he added. My father went along for the ride—quite unaware that he would be included as a driver in the hectic goose roundup.

"There they are. Help yourselves," said the farmer, waving his hand toward a high-fenced patch of alfalfa. "Just don't go near the pair nesting in that corner or the other pair over there." He indicated two general locations. "Sorry I couldn't catch them for you, but I'll give you a hand in sacking them if you bring them over here," he added.

Dad and I put on our raincoats, grabbed two nets, and started through the knee-high alfalfa. The cagey Canadas knew we were after them. They either froze close to the ground or took off like scared rabbits. One by one, we cornered them or ran them down.

47

We then had to lug them over to the corner near the driveway where the farmer lifted them by their necks over the fence and into gunny sacks cut to allow the heads to protrude.

Nesting on a construction site

After an hour, nine Canadas were in the truck bound for their new home. What that generous farmer didn't know was that another pair of mated geese was included in our catch. At least, within a few weeks, we witnessed the astonishing behavior of the Canada geese building a nest on the remains of the Old Duck Island. This was right in the middle of the construction of the New Duck Islands when the bulldozers were pushing out the dumped earth fill toward the fifth and last of the new islands.

This determined lady Canada had established her nest right on top of the biggest heap of dirt on the Old Island. When discovered, she had already laid one egg. The gander, her devoted

Canada goose.

mate, shared her determination. They lowered their heads, hissed, and threatened to take on the bulldozer and startled operator.

The bulldozer operator, being human and sentimental about things like that, was easily persuaded to leave that heap and work elsewhere until the Canadas hatched their eggs. They readily appeared to understand the truce because they took turns at their precious nest and didn't get too excited as the bulldozers plowed past.

Many a Canada goose family has been brought ashore since that time. Nowadays, by March, at least eight nests are going on the five islands. The noisy and argumentative pairs will very sensibly divide the larger islands into individual territories wherein each can enter and leave its nest site without disturbing their neighbors. The score or more of one- or two-year-old unmated Canadas which just hang around quickly take the hint to stay away from these nest locations. The pushy mallard hens, however, may be allowed to nest within a few feet of the honkers.

Six to nine fluffy, yellow goslings are proudly led ashore by each pair between mid-April and early May. Right up the sloping parts of the retaining walls, they bravely follow their parents. While the goose and gander graze on their favorite lawn strip a few feet from passing pedestrians, cyclists, and whizzing traffic, the goslings forage for tiny bugs and the tenderest bits of greens. Bird lovers coming suddenly upon this scene may swoon. Residents of the nearby high-rise apartments become their self-appointed patrons and guardians.

As a second, third, or fourth newly-hatched family joins the flock, past arguments over nesting territories are forgotten. Look-out duties are assumed in turn by a certain number of the parents. Appearance of a dog-walker or small boys with sticks starts the pairs toward the water, scolding and herding along the reluctant goslings.

If the dog or person comes on too fast or too close, watch for trouble. The gander may turn, extend his neck, ruffle his feathers, and charge like a fury. When close enough, he will raise a wing and strike the adversary. I have seen dogs and small children sent reeling over backwards. Rarely do they return for another bout with the gander.

These same cautious Canada parents, though quick to anger, are also quick to recognize their real friends. Those who sit quietly

Roundup of young Canada Geese for banding.

on the grass with proper handouts soon find themselves closely
surrounded by the Canadas and their broods.

Fluffy goslings soon turn into lanky, greyish offspring. But
parental devotion and solicitude remains unrelenting. Only after
some weeks are the youngsters permitted to venture short dis-
tances from the family circle. It is the eighth or ninth week from
hatching before the youngsters find themselves with wings developed enough for short flights across the water. And about that
time, father and mother have lost their flight pinions in the
summer eclipse moult and are grounded!

Geese offspring, like human children, must eventually grow
up, mate, and leave home. The Duck Islands could not accomodate
the population explosion of Canadas. The flock of fifty-five to
eighty that grazed on Park lawns in winter suddenly thinned to
half that number toward spring. Where had they gone? Some
we had banded before they could fly, but at first, we heard little
from them. Then the reports began to come in.

"We have Canada geese nesting here in our back yard. Could
they be yours from Lake Merritt?" asked an excited voice over
the phone. The caller lived on the South Shore man-made lagoons
in Alameda.

They were ours, we assumed, as they wore rather new bands. We drove over to check on this report and found a group of honkers cruising up and down the Alameda lagoons.

The next report came from Brooks Island off Richmond. The gun club caretaker there actually brought us a snapshot of our banded nesting Canadas.

And so the nine honkers from that farmer's pasture have grown into a thriving colony that promises to populate the East-bay shores.

Godfrey and Gwendolyn

Godfrey was just another member of the goose watchers at the Duck Pond until the Gwendolyn incident which occurred suddenly and without warning. Godfrey burst into the office in a state of great distress, "Gwen is staggering. She can't stand. Please, come right away. We must do something. I want to pay for any treatment she needs!"

"Who is Gwen?" we asked in some bewilderment.

"Gwen is my Chinese goose," snapped Godfrey with some impatience. "She's a wonderful, affectionate bird, and she must be saved. I'll take her to a veterinarian myself or do anything you say."

"Let's go," I said. We hadn't notice anything seriously wrong with any of the geese, but this man was not in a mood for denial or postponement.

Sure enough, there was Gwen having a rough time just staying upright on the floor of his car. "You pick her up," I directed, "and put her in this empty pen while I phone a vet."

I selected a pet clinic that we knew performed occasional bird salvage jobs. The young assistant vet who answered the phone indicated considerable empathy for cases like this. "We have a man and a goose who both need attention, Doc, and I'm not sure which is the more serious," I said.

"Send them right up, and we will do the best we can. We're always treating cases like your friend by treating their pets as well." I dashed out to inform Godfrey that the pet clinic would take his case right away.

An hour later Godfrey returned displaying obvious relief and satisfaction. "Look," he beamed, thrusting a paper into my hands, "they not only fixed up Gwen, but they were very reasonable."

The clinic's office treatment statement looked very professional: antibiotics, an injection containing familiar diarrhea control, and dosages of capsules to be given orally over a period of several days. Total charge: $12.50.

That was quite reasonable, we all agreed (since our friend was paying the bill). Then we asked as an after-thought "Where is Gwen? Are they holding her overnight for observation?"

"Oh no, Gwen is outside in my car," Godfrey assured us. I'm going to have to get her out right away. She made quite a mess of the cushions."

We allowed Gwen's friend to transfer his patient back to the Duck Pond enclosure. We didn't have the heart to look at his car because we should have remembered to give him a box to carry Gwen to the clinic.

"Gwen can stand. In fact she can walk quite well again. They certainly got her in time and knew just what to do," Godfrey assured us at about closing time that afternoon. "But I'll have to come down at least twice a day for her medications. They are very important. And we'll have to coax Gwen out on the lawn to eat more grass. Some of this food other people give her just isn't good."

Godfrey was true to his word. Two or three times each day he was out there with his vials, leaning over the fence to administer to Gwen. He said he had to close his place of business each time he left, but he never complained about that little detail. And a few days later we happened to be watching when Gwen drove off a big mute swan who dared approach her friend.

Put down that goose!

Godfrey would readily reprimand the person who dared lay hands on Gwen, according to an incident reported to us the very next week. In fact we wondered if this mild-mannered fellow might not be a Jekyll-Hyde type who could suddenly see red and commit mayhem upon anyone abusing a goose, duck, swan, or any other bird.

It seems that one evening when Godfrey was nearby, two male visitors accompanied by children made the grievous error of stuffing Gwen with pieces of bread. Gwen was greedy and accepted these bread chunks too fast and developed a bulky food-jam in her esophagus. Then one of the male visitors seized her by the neck and tried to massage down the obstructing food.

The unfortunate man lacked proper techniques in goose handling. Gwen squawked in muffled distress and Godfrey came running. "Put down that goose," he ordered.

But the stranger held on and continued his crude efforts to relieve Gwen. Thereupon Gwen's protector hauled off and socked the man in the chest. This finally convinced the man that he should leave Gwen to her own devices. Fortunately for Godfrey, both visitors withdrew instead of making a real brawl out of it.

When we heard about all this, we remonstrated gently with Godfrey. "Couldn't you have argued with the fellows or threatened to call the rangers?" we asked. "You know we couldn't defend you for hitting a stranger unless he first threatened you."

This he knew, he admitted, but he was still going to do anything necessary to protect Gwen or any other bird. Then to change the subject, he produced a couple of new vials of medication he had just secured to follow up Gwen's treatment.

Godfrey also developed a special fondness for a people-oriented brown Chinese goose that he called Christine. He knew who brought the goose to the Park, and he had personally assured them he would protect and comfort their unwanted pet.

Christine adored and clung to certain people, and to Godfrey most of all, to a degree that made the bird a major problem around the Duck Pond. As the last of its regular friends left the Park at the end of each afternoon, Christine would stand at the curb, or even out in the street, protesting loudly. Godfrey would return

later each evening to feed and comfort his special pet, and I presume the goose remembered that.

I became so harassed by the spectacle of Christine calling pitifully as we closed each evening, and by Godfrey's constant fretting over the bird, that I suggested he sometimes take it home overnight. Godfrey jumped at this offer with only some mutterings about his car and his landlord. I called my superior to get an official O.K. for this extraordinary arrangement.

Despite all this, none of us was quite prepared for the sight that greeted one of our staff as Godfrey drove into the Park one Sunday morning. There he was driving his convertible with the top down and with someone wearing a gay straw bonnet in the seat beside him. This interested the Park employee, as Godfrey usually drove alone. He managed to overtake Godfrey to satisfy his curiosity. The passenger was Christine trying to keep its place in the front seat and to shake off the unwelcome headgear!

All the while we suspected that Christine was a gander. On occasions when Christine showed some interest in the other Chinese geese, its behavior was definitely that of a male.

This problem goose had attracted the attention of two of the Fairyland gardeners who were having goose social problems of their own. They had what they described as a lonely female Chinese goose. They put in a request for Godfrey's pet as a companion for her.

Dreading another difficult scene, I hesitantly broached this proposition to Godfrey. Perhaps he was getting tired of hauling his noisy sloppy Chinese goose back and forth. Yes, he agreed, a term at Fairyland might be the right thing for "her."

Then I told Godfrey that his pet was really a gander and would be a companion to a female Chinese goose. Henceforth, Christine would be called Chris. This news did shake Godfrey quite visibly!

Chris was established in Fairyland. He did keep company with the Chinese female, but to the extreme chagrin of the matchmakers, he appeared to want it a platonic friendship.

Goose lovers vs. the establishment

Before very long the Fairyland personnel were complaining about Godfrey and certain other goose lovers who insisted on following their beloved bird into Fairyland. They claimed that

54

Chris didn't receive the proper diet. Even on the days when Fairy-land was closed, Godfrey would come bright and early to the gate with his heads of lettuce, and call back and forth to Chris. Fairy-land had always boasted its "Mother Goose" characters who worked in various capacities there, but they hadn't bargained for this eccentric "goose man" and associates who entered the Fairy-land scene.

I know of a nearby park agency that managed to arrange the sale of their surplus domestic ducks and geese to a local market. This provided extra revenue for special facilities for children's play-grounds. The only hangups in this convenient arrangement were certain park frequenters like Godfrey who developed emotional attachments to particular birds. Such a goose protector on their local scene was Gus.

Gus became deeply attached to some French Toulouse geese living on the park pond. Then spring brought mating, nesting, and offspring. The goslings were numerous and healthy, and soon grew too big for that particular pond and park. Some just had to go, the supervisors decided.

Several of the geese were rounded up and put in a holding pen for the market truck to pick up. But Gus came by first.

Gus knew the fate of domestic birds that landed in the pen. This must not happen to *his* pets. He had worked himself into quite a state of panic by the time he located the park supervisor. He had also telephoned the S.P.C.A. and the local press!

"They mustn't be killed. They mustn't be sold for eating. Why can't I buy them? I have a friend who will give them a home. I'll even pay their board bill if necessary," Gus pleaded with the park man.

Then the park supervisor offered this solution. "Look, Gus," he said, "why don't you get down to the market about the time the guy gets there with the geese and offer to buy them right there? You know we can't sell them to you or any citizen, but we would like to see them get a new home instead of landing in someone's oven."

Gus went for this like the lawyer who is offered a deal to keep his client from going to Death Row. He gushed forth thanks and blessings for the embarrassed supervisor, then dashed off to phone his friend with "the home in the suburbs" to summon her help to rescue the geese and carry them to her yard.

55

Just to be sure there were no tragic errors to frustrate this amicable arrangement, the supervisor telephoned the market. They were delighted to unload this oversize poultry at the curb at any price they cared to ask.

The goose protector didn't take any chances. He stationed his friend at the market while he waited for the truck, watched them pick up the protesting gray geese, then followed it closely to the market.

I would like to report that they all lived happily forever afterward, but that wouldn't be entirely true. A couple of the young Toulouse, ungrateful Frenchmen that they were, soon walked out of their new home and took off across suburbia. Gus and his friend drove and walked miles around the nearby neighborhoods asking various residents if they had seen some stray gray geese. Yes, they had been seen, but nobody had stopped them because they acted as if they knew where they were going.

Sometime during the next day the runaways were located. They had actually waddled their merry way down the hill, across streets, and through yards and vacant lots until they arrived at Lake Temescal—a nice place with a children's day-care center.

Now Gus had to confront another park supervisor. People swam at one end of this lake, and the health inspectors frowned on humans sharing water with waterfowl. Something about a salmonella organism, they claimed. But, with the vociferous pleading of the children's center who promised to keep the geese on their end of the lake, they won another reprieve. They wouldn't have to be returned to the new home they scorned nor to the horrible fate of the market!

Apartment-dwelling goose

Another favored and fortunate goose—a full-grown fat Toulouse—lived in a comfortable flat high above Lake Merritt. When her foster parents, Pat and Glenn, allowed her to look out the front windows, she could observe her kinfolk crossing the lawns and grazing on common grass, in company with the flocks of native geese, ducks, and other birds.

"Donna" was found as an "ugly gosling," of uncertain parentage. She came ashore with Canada geese in the spring of 1967. She didn't quite resemble the cute, yellow Canada goslings she tried to follow, and still she didn't look exactly like the Toulouse goslings which hatched about the same time. And neither Canada nor Toulouse parents really wanted her.

Pat, a lovely young woman quite devoted to the birds, spent many daylight hours around the Duck Pond and the lake while Glenn was at work, and she fell for this unloved, unwanted gosling. With our ready permission, she took it home to their nearby flat to coddle and rear.

This ugly gosling must have displayed some characteristics that caused her foster parents to call her "Don." Anyhow, they assumed her to be a male. They proceeded to turn over their comfortable flat to "his" convenience. The bathtub was put at the youngster's disposal night and morning. But Don couldn't properly dry himself until he could get out of the tub to ruffle and shake his few juvenile feathers and shed water in all directions. Pat or Glenn tried to be on hand with an ample bath towel to soak up some of the child's spongy plumage before this happened.

At the age of eight weeks when this waif finally acquired most of its juvenile plumage, it became apparent that Don was a young Toulouse goose. This meant that it would soon surpass any Canada goose in weight, appetite, and even vocal talents. This

APT. for Rent

NO PETS

began to worry Pat and Glenn a little. They tried carrying the gosling over to the Duck Pond to meet some of its relatives — perhaps its own indifferent parents. But this orphan didn't look like one of their offspring. The Duck Pond Toulouse geese showed disdain toward it, and one or two even hissed menacingly.

So back to the flat went Don. It appeared its outdoor life would be limited to the small lawn and garden belonging to the apartment house. This he seemed to enjoy when Pat and Glenn took "him" downstairs in the early evening. But even this contact with nature outdoors was to be denied the gosling.

A neighbor's dog spotted Don and set up a roar at this strange creature in the garden. Other neighbors looked out to find the cause of all the barking. One of them had to be a busybody who immediately saw cause for alarm over this unusual pet and phoned the Health Department demanding they do something about this goose-in-a-house.

Fortunately, Pat and Glenn received a warning. When the Health Inspector arrived during regular business hours, Don was back in his secure flat, and Pat and Glenn were both away. Nobody would say exactly which flat the offensive bird occupied, so the Inspector gave up and went away.

Pat and Glenn should have suspected their mistake in naming their "goose child" when Don showed such constant attachment to Glenn, following him everywhere around the flat. It particularly liked to share the shaving soap when Glenn shaved. It showed great distaste for the stuff, spitting and shaking it off its head, but it always returned for more. This threw doubts on Don's intelligence.

The plain facts of the goose-child's sex were suddenly revealed as Don neared his first birthday. "He" began to lay an egg a day. Pat and Glenn were somewhat dismayed until they decided to try one for breakfast. It was delicious and almost big enough for two. So "Donna" began to pay for her keep.

No geese need apply

A traumatic event occurred in the lives of Donna and her foster parents early in the fall of 1968. Glenn was suddenly transferred to the Los Angeles area, and given very short notice to find a residence down there and to move the "family."

Donna, being an indispensible part of the family, presented the major problem. When Pat and Glenn began searching for an acceptable home in Los Angeles, they found "No Pets" posted in the nicer apartment houses. They asked a few landlords if a goose fell in this category and got an emphatic *"Yes!"* In fact, two or three landlords responded so emphatically that they got the idea that a big gray goose was about the last thing any property owner would think of having.

That is how Donna eventually found herself established in a lovely one-story home with a spacious patio, located high in the cool, clear Palos Verdes Hills above the smoggy Los Angeles Basin. Pat and Glenn simply bought a home fit for a proud and discerning gray goose. But there's quite a story about how Donna got to her new home.

A boarding place had to be found for Donna when Pat and Glenn got into the business of packing. Even if they had wanted to carry their pet directly to her new home, they realized she wouldn't fit well into their little European-model car. At least, a proper crate wouldn't fit, and even the most enthusiastic goose lover generally draws the line at transporting live geese unboxed in the family car.

Fortunately, a friend in a suburban community came to the rescue. She would gladly board Donna until her new home was properly prepared. Glenn's company would pay, of course, since Donna was one of the family.

A few weeks later Donna's home was ready. A deluxe crate, built for both comfort and security, was designed for air travel to Los Angeles. Donna's sitter personally delivered the goose into the airport's custody to avoid any possible delays or rough handling by pick-up trucks. After all, Glenn had assured her that his company wanted no reasonable expense spared in getting this goose-child to its new home.

And so it was that Donna arrived in good condition at her spacious Palos Verdes home, though extremely disturbed over the business of being in a crate and attended by strange humans. In subsequent years Donna followed Pat and Glenn to new homes in Texas and New Jersey—and continued to supply fresh eggs!

Ichabod Crane comes to Oakland

One morning the staff greeted me with unaccustomed excitement. "There's a surprise for you over in the dome cage, Paul. Our prize bird came in over the weekend," announced Mr. Kett. "Better get over there and meet it."

"What prize bird?" I demanded. Some of these prize birds unexpectedly given to us turn out to be lemons.

"It's the crane," filled in George. "Don't you remember the sandhill crane the Fish and Wildlife Service promised to bring here when the wildlife film was completed?"

"You mean the sandhill crane is here?" I echoed. I started across the feeding area toward the dome.

A strident trumpeting greeted us as we approached the dome cage. And there he stood, drawn up to his full commanding stature, peering at us through the mesh—a magnificent sandhill crane. His red cap and white cheeks contrasted sharply with his otherwise sleek gray neck and body plumage. Only some slightly twisted primary (outer wing joint) pinions detracted from his regal appearance.

"The fellows who left him said they thought his bent wings were the result of artificial feeding when he was growing up," commented George. "He can still fly a little because they had him flying alongside their car when they were making the film."

"Let's call him 'Ichabod'." That name to me had always suggested someone tall and gawky (no reference to any living person intended).

George, carrying some tidbit he thought the crane would like, let himself into the Dome, but I noticed that he had picked up a bamboo gravel-rake which he kept carefully between himself and Ichabod. This fine bird did boast a ten-inch spear-like bill which he held in a menacing ready position. If he chose to jab you in the eye, it would be too late to start guessing his intentions. This time he took the tidbit off the palm of George's hand without puncturing it. Perhaps his looks belied his actions.

This bird was abandoned by its parents on the Malheur National Wildlife Refuge in southeastern Oregon. Sandhill cranes have a strange incubation schedule which often results in serious disruptions in rearing their small families.

The sandhill female lays two eggs a couple of days apart, but begins incubating at once. The chicks then hatch a few days apart. The first one to hatch is taken afield by the concerned father to forage, while mother stays with her nest vigil. When the second chick tumbles out of its shell and dries off, she leads it off in the general direction of father and the first-born. Unfortunately the devoted parents often try to keep the chicks apart during the daylight feeding hours. All this leads to social problems

60

Gosling 'nappers—Canada goose pair and "borrowed" brood with their own.

Ichabod Crane takes snack from special friend, Rex Burress.

when one of the crane children frequently strays and is abandoned. We presumed that Ichabod was just such an unfortunate bird.

The next day I headed into the Dome Aviary with both still and movie cameras. Ichabod didn't need much coaxing to dance and trumpet. His outbursts were almost ear-splitting at close range. People hurried to the Dome Cage and were amazed to find a mere bird producing such sounds. They confessed they thought we had a young elephant.

It didn't take long to get pictures of Ichabod dancing. There isn't much space on the little gravel beach in the Dome Aviary, but a crane doesn't necessarily require much space to dance. Ichabod's vertical leaps from a standing position were prodigious. They easily brought him over a man's head since he stood four feet high to begin with. He responded most enthusiastically to Rex Burress, the keeper with particular rapport with new bird and mammal arrivals.

Troublemaker in Paradise

Then I observed this fine bird from outside the Dome Cage. What I saw was most disturbing. Ichabod had upset the entire social order of that big cage.

The duck and goose inhabitants of the Dome and even the ring-necked pheasants and the bold Brandt cormorant all gave this new giant a wide berth. As Ichabod spent much of his time standing in the center of the cage, this was a real problem. He was willing and ready to lunge with his bill at any bird that dared venture into that area. Even the small pool afforded slight refuge to these dispossessed fowl, as the crane could wade out to its knee joints and from that position menace the entire pool with his sweeping reach. Only when something lured Ichabod into the outer periphery of the cage could the other occupants approach the central area.

But there was a challenge to this new usurper. It came from overhead where Ichabod could not reach the comparative midgets who dared take him on. There was a mated pair of sparrow hawks or kestrels when Ichabod entered the Dome in April. This pair and the other three unmated kestrels regarded this long-legged monster as a threat to their security. They were particularly disturbed when choice bits of ground meat were handed to Ichabod just before their feeding. The kestrels' chopped chicken head meals were

tossed up and deftly caught on the wing. This also left the crane
out of the picture and considerably disturbed him too.

So Ichabod was harrassed by aerial dives, feints, and shrill
screams by these agile little falcons. He leaped toward them with
open wings and extended neck, but his powerful bill always
snapped shut some inches from the darting hawks. It was a great
act. Finally the kestrels lost interest in the affair. It appeared the
monster was there to stay. And besides, the nesting project of the
mated pair fizzled out.

Ichabod lived in the Dome for many weeks. Although he remained hostile toward all the other bird occupants, they did seem
to find enough opportunity to reach their food. During the feeding
performance, George or Rex found ways of getting the fish to the
cormorant and some black-crowned night herons and the meat to
the kestrels, without any damaging encounters between men or
birds. And the crane's leaps and trumpetings continued to high-
light the feeding show in the Dome.

But citizen observers kept bringing disturbing reports of
Ichabod stabbing certain ducks and smaller birds. Yet none of the
staff actually saw him doing this. Then one day we caught him in
the act. Habitual law breakers become overconfident and careless,
they say.

Alerted by a bystander's excited report, the bird keeper
hurried to the Dome and found Ichabod repeatedly stabbing a
small teal duck. The bird was beyond feeling any further pain, but
the crane was playing with it as a cat plays with a mouse.

That was enough to convince me. Ichabod had to leave the
big aviary. Display specimens like teal, wood ducks, mandarins,
and others in that collection were too hard to come by. Much as
we loved to show off Ichabod in the large waterfowl cage, we
couldn't turn it over to him.

Ichabod is banished

So the sandhill crane was moved into the spacious "banding
roundup trap." There he could stretch his legs but had to get used
to a seven foot ceiling when he felt like dancing. The closest the
public could approach him was a fence some forty feet away, but
he commanded a full view of the hundreds of ducks, scores of
geese, and flocks of tame pigeons that used the feeding area
throughout the day.

This transfer to private quarters didn't cure Ichabod of his bird-spearing instincts. One day we found him with a pigeon which had innocently ventured too close to his wire boundaries; another day he managed to get a luckless duckling. He never ate his victims. Perhaps he stalked them because boredom led him into such pursuits.

Most of the Duck Pond birds learned to stay clear of Ichabod's quarters. This situation presented a serious obstacle to regular operations, as this big trap was used to round up surplus pigeons, hybrid mallards and Pekins, and would be used to catch some ducks for banding in the winter season. On pigeon-trapping days, we tried rigging a temporary roll of mesh to confine the crane to the lower corner of the cage, but the wily pigeons remained suspicious.

I felt sorry for this boisterous, people-oriented bird in spite of his criminal tendencies. I made a habit of calling to him and walking over to his cage with little snacks or gifts. Food snacks were not really necessary to rouse Ichabod to a song-and-dance mood. A bright-petaled flower, a piece of rag or paper, even the pinions shed by other birds—any of these donations was enough to send him into ecstasy. His subsequent trumpeting would draw immediate attention from visitors and would lead to questions about this solitary captive in the big pen.

Feathered ham actors like Ichabod and the white pelicans placed in our custody by the Bureau of Sport Fisheries and Wildlife accomplish much more than visitor entertainment. Ichabod's wild kinfolk, the sandhill cranes that gather during the winter in California's Great Valley, may not be in immediate danger of extinction. But their famous cousin, the whooping crane, barely survives as a wild species on this continent. Its wintering grounds on the Texas Gulf Coast are threatened by commercial developments, and it must fly a long, dangerous course yearly to its remote Canadian breeding grounds. Experiments with raising the more common orphaned sandhills like Ichabod have helped federal researchers at Patuxent, Maryland, to hatch and rear whooping cranes in captivity.

The agonizing problems, the successes and failures dedicated men encounter in trying to save America's endangered wildlife species, and how interested citizens could assist in these efforts, were presented to Lake Merritt visitors while they admired such a prize example as Ichabod.

It is indeed fortunate that we can still tell them: "If you want to see and hear cranes by the hundreds, go to the Grey Lodge State Waterfowl Management Area in the Sacramento Valley. You'll find them feeding, dancing, and soaring there—right next to tens of thousands of ducks and geese. We hope they may still be there when your children grow up!"

Bird Watchers: Amateurs to Pros

Are you a frustrated bird watcher, perhaps with a rich potential for self-discovery so far untapped? Do you secretly peek through the curtains and admire those dynamic little creatures you've fed in your garden or on your window sill but hesitate to get further involved because you've never been properly introduced? Are you shy about joining the flocks of your fellow countrymen of all ages and backgrounds who have discovered a new world of recreation, friends, and amazing facts in the pursuit of their feathered neighbors and others far afield?

If I've correctly diagnosed your trouble, my Bashful Bird Watcher, I can easily prescribe the cure. If you are fortunate enough to live in an area where there is an Audubon chapter or other bird club, take your spouse, friend, or young ones (better to start them early) and show up at the starting point of the next field trip. No dogs, please. I can promise you a warm welcome.

A most exciting and rewarding time to join your local bird group would be a spring nesting survey. It would help if you already knew or could take a crash course in identifying the common year-round birds of your area. Otherwise, attempting to identify all the spring and summer arrivals in some localities, even with a guide, could send you home in shock!

The Audubon Christmas Census

The generation gap and the polarization of age groups so bitterly decried in North American society today is hard to detect when the bird chasers, the serious students, and the neophytes get together for one of these all-out efforts. The most exciting of these concerted undertakings is also the most publicized because it involves a competition that embraces all of the United States and the Canadian provinces.

The Audubon Christmas Count started in 1900 with twenty-seven persons counting birds in twenty-five localities, mostly in the eastern United States. Now a typical Christmas Count involves as many as 30,000 birders reporting on more than 1200 areas in the United States and Canada. This army of spotters and counters must carry out its mission within a two-week period centered around Christmas. Each local society selects a date, then undertakes to identify and count birds within a carefully drawn territory not over fifteen miles in diameter.

There must be a mastermind behind each such operation, and this "field marshal" is known as the "compiler." A census team in arctic Alaska or the frigid Canadian prairie country may consist simply of a man and wife, while a compiler directing a census along the coast of California, Florida, or the Texas gulf may have to organize over one hundred participants. Each large task force must be split into teams, a responsible leader found for each team, and the territory carefully divided among these teams.

A start at daybreak is a standing order, come sunshine, flood rains, or blizzard. But an eight-, nine-, or ten-hour day isn't sufficient for some compilers and territories. There are those night birds to be included if you're going to do the job right. Let's have some volunteers for owl calling. Young people will always go for this. Doctor Smith will go along—he's an authority on owl voices and doesn't mind getting up in the night. Set your alarms for three a.m., everybody. You should get the screech, saw-whet, and great horned (all owls) if you work it right!

One December pre-dawn the chill fog lay heavy in the canyons and the owls didn't respond, no matter how the experts hooted, and trilled, and squeaked. A nervous housewife did respond, however, and the owl callers suddenly found themselves surrounded by the police. A middle-aged male birder who was persuaded to join an owling task force had to be evacuated from the front lines to his home to be tucked under warm blankets and given strong libations before he could return at a more reasonable hour to carry on with the daytime census.

Then there is the marine arm of operation "bird count" where the census territory includes bays or offshore waters. The boat may be borrowed or rented from the local Sea Scouts or a friendly commercial fisherman. A hand-picked commando party of Audubonites who know their water birds and can take offshore weather is selected for this duty. A very successful census "bag" on San Francisco Bay, for example, would net three species of loons, a red-necked grebe, and strays from ocean waters such as a jaegar or skua, some petrels, an auklet, or a murre.

There is the marsh, beach, and tidelands contingent. They, too, must often compete with obscuring fogs or bitter winds, the roar of jets from adjacent airports, or "keep out" signs where new subdivisions are usurping bird habitats. Here real experts in identification and estimating numbers are also required. Those pesky sandpipers, for example, numbering into the hundreds, huddle in tightly-packed phalanxes on solid ground at high tide, then fan out across acres of mudflats at low tide. And how do you count accurately those rafts of diving ducks that bob up and down on the choppy waters?

A small lake or pond is a much better place to initiate beginners in this bird-counting business. The raw recruit can be given the mallards, mud hens, and blackbirds in the adjacent marsh to tabulate. Even the unfortunate birder confined to a set of crutches can participate if there happens to be a road around the place.

Lake Merritt and the waterfowl refuge were made to order for the birder of limited experience or severe physical handicap. I've always welcomed these people at the Christmas Count, and we've never run out of the "easy species" for them to count. But the lake offers many stickier problems of bird-spotting as well, such as distinguishing six or seven different gulls and their mottled immature phases, three or four kinds of grebes, and a rare drop-in duck like the Tufted duck which might well be the only one of its kind on any western Christmas Count!

Even the stay-at-home who watches a bird-feeding station through the window may contribute a rare observation to the census. It may be an Eastern white-throated sparrow or a wintering black-headed grosbeak at Berkeley, California—a dickcissel or white-winged crossbill at Springfield, Massachusetts—or a rufous hummingbird or Western meadowlark in Pensacola, Florida. Binoculars, careful identification, and a telephone are all that are required to put that shut-in bird watcher on the hero list for the day.

When the Count is over

When darkness falls all too soon on Christmas Count day, and each counter must holster his binoculars, lay away his telescope, and fold his notebook crammed with names and figures, what then? Why, there has to be a roundup of birders to tally the results of the day's effort.

And who will receive this tired, hungry army of census-takers? It may be the local school, club hall, or grange. Tanks of hot coffee and heaps of sandwiches may be sent over by those who did not get into the field. And many a home is thrown open to the Christmas Count birders—even if they numbered three score and ten, like one East Bay task force a few years ago. There they were— all ages, sizes, conditions of dress, complexions, hair lengths, and hair styles. It was just too much for the friendly family dog who had to be removed to the back yard!

Everyone awaits expectantly the "moment of truth," no matter how good the food and drink or how stimulating the company. This comes when the compiler calls the gathering to order. Team leaders get out their lists for the day. A hush falls.

The compiler holds up his master list. For Northern California birders, the field check list is *The Birds of the Pacific States.*

"Common loon," he intones, "who got the common loon?"

"Here, yeah," call out the team leaders.

He goes through the loons and the grebes, with every species reported; then comes the albatross, fulmar, shearwaters, and petrels, all offshore or ocean-going birds.

Here he draws a prolonged, agonizing silence, until a voice pipes up from the far corner of the room.

"One Leach's petrel sighted from our boat off the Berkeley Yacht Harbor," announces a heavily-bearded youth seated on the floor and still swathed in a corduroy jacket.

The tally proceeds with appropriate remarks and exclamations—even an occasional "amen" when a rarer species is brought into the roundup by the "yeah" of a single voice.

The overly eager youngster or inexperienced grownup who reports sighting a rare golden eagle or a stray yellow-shafted flicker may get himself into a friendly cross-examination. He'd have done better to report it first and discuss it with his team leader, if he saw his rare bird while all alone in the field. Otherwise he is in for considerable embarrassment, at the least. At the worst, he may be demoted to counting unmistakable species on the next census, like mud hens on Lake Merritt.

Christmas Bird Count rules as set forth by the editor of *Audubon's American Birds* specify that "If birds unusual for your area around Christmas are reported, a sheet must accompany the report giving satisfactory details of such observations." Moreover, the initials of the observer or observers must be printed beside the record.

I was somewhat startled at the evening tally following a recent count to find a leading California ornithologist carefully filling out a sheet for a "rare species sighting," with all kinds of intimate details including the reporter's background. It was for a peregrine falcon—one of the vanishing American birds of prey.

Within an hour, crammed with surprise records and inexplicable drop-outs or "no-shows" of certain species, the tally nears its climax as the compiler reaches the sparrows and finches on the master list.

The telephone rings in the next room. The host answers and soon bursts into the living room with good news.

"That was Mrs. B——. The white-throated sparrow was on her feeding tray this afternoon!" (This species is a rare stray on the Pacific coast.)

The grand total of species for the day is already being figured by a sharp young lady. This is the real "moment of truth" that all await.

"One hundred and sixty-one!" announces the lady in not very joyful tones. A moan runs through the audience. The East Bay count has sometimes scored over one hundred and seventy.

"Hey, suppose I run down to Lakeside Park and try to get a barn owl?" suggests one of the teenagers.

"Fine," agrees the compiler. "And maybe we'll still hear from Joe who went after the long-eared owls in the canyon." The Christmas Count time period runs until midnight.

"One thing's for sure," observes a veteran birder, "we'll never make one of the top four lists. The Point Reyes people may make it. I had a call from one of them at seven o'clock—said they'd get a list of 190 or better. They're headed to beat San Diego or Cocoa, Florida." (Both of these areas regularly score above 200 species.)

Compiling the returns

The weary birders return to their homes when all the counting is over, but not the compiler. His responsibilities shift from organization and direction to tabulations. Totals of individual species must be taken from each field card handed in, added and set down on a master form. The mileage put in by each counter team, by foot, auto, or boat, must also be added and listed. The correct names and addresses of each birder must be recorded and every name must be matched by a fee if it is to be printed in *Audubon's American Birds* Christmas Count issue.

All this data must be accurately recorded on those master report forms furnished by the editor of Audubon's "American Birds" and returned by January 15, or risk being lost forever as far as national publication goes. You will readily understand why bird counters come back year after year, but far less often do compilers.

Some startling revelations of bird movements, concentrations, and other phenomena are brought to light as a result of these Christmas Counts. Such was the case of hordes of robins invading the city of Oakland by its back door, so to speak. In some past years, they came by tens of thousands—officially undetected and undeclared—while the bird counters faithfully watched and counted only the hundreds which commuted daily from city parks and front yards to their nightly roost in Palos Colorados Canyon. Why didn't the birders look a little farther and discover the big flocks?

The robin is a bird whose general welfare and population level has been boosted incalculably by civilization and the spread of subdivisions, city parks, and even freeways. Every new home,

71

park, playground, and public building means a fresh piece of lawn and new berried bushes. Even highway landscapers planted berried shrubs by the thousands until the mass killing of berry-drunk robins by passing traffic aroused the bird lovers.

Add the normally mild winter weather along the coast of California and the Pacific northwest to these new sources of food and you have a veritable paradise for Robin Redbreast, which is shared to a much lesser degree by flocks of cedar waxwings and other berry-eaters.

California has a rather large summer population of robins which nest all the way from the coast to the high Sierra and move to lower elevations or southward in the fall. If the winter is mild and wild berries like the toyon and madrone are plentiful, their kinfolk up in Oregon, Washington, and British Columbia may not bother to come south to visit the California robin paradise. During such seasons, Bay Region bird watchers become greatly concerned and call park naturalists, museums, and newspapers to demand what has happened to the robins. Have pesticides got them?

Birders and bird watchers in action at Alameda South Shore.

But just let a violent November or December storm with widespread freezing and heavy snows sweep across the Pacific northwest, and the robin invasion is on. Robins swarm in every city park and neighborhood that offers berry bushes and lawns. The robin-lovers are assured and happy. Now it is the robin-haters who begin calling.

"What can I do about these filthy birds? They gobble up my neighbor's red berries, and then they decorate my clothesline. What will drive them away?"

"This is Attorney Brown of Brown, Bemiss, Bloom and Schultz calling for our client, the manufacturing plant at 10 Frontage Road. The damn birds are gorging on those berry bushes you planted down here, and they're defecating all over the walks, and the employees' and customers' cars. If you don't get the birds or the bushes out of here, we're going to file a claim. . . ." And so the hassles go on.

Palos Colorados Robin Roost

But something much more exciting is taking place in the hills above Oakland. The great evening spectacle of homing and social massing at the Palos Colorados Robin Roost is on again!

Nobody seems to know how far back this roost got started. My first tip-offs came from backyard bird watchers on the hills who called the park naturalist about the numbers of birds streaming over their homes toward sundown. That's how we discovered the robins by the *tens of thousands* coming from Contra Costa County and passing over many other potential roosts to join the East Bay robins in this particular canyon . . . only to rise at sunup and fly back to their widespread daytime foraging areas.

Beautiful Palos Colorados Canyon lies along an earthquake fault in Joaquin Miller Park in the Oakland Hills. Second-growth coast redwoods grow along the canyon bottom on Palos Colorados Creek, while the north-facing slope is heavily clothed in California bay or laurel trees—the aromatic evergreens that thrive in cool canyons along the Pacific coast. A small, once-bare hilltop that overlooks the canyon is crowned by one of the stone monuments built by the poet Joaquin Miller who, in the eighties, settled on this hillside overlooking San Francisco Bay. Tall *eucalypti,* Monterey pines, and cypresses, originally planted by Joaquin and

73

friends, crowd these slopes and the much higher ones across
the canyon.

Robins by the thousands were streaming through the sky and
flowing down over the Skyline Boulevard forest that late afternoon in December when I along with some birder friends became
aware of this phenomenon. Some birds paused for brief rests on
the higher branches of the *eucalypti* for conversation with their
associates, then plunged down into the protective canopy of the
bay trees to their overnight roosting perches. Small flocks of waxwings flitted back and forth among the robins. The sinister figure
of a Cooper hawk was soon among the top branches of a tree,
watching the robins but hesitant to strike. Late straggler flocks of
robins were silhouetted against a fiery winter sun, settling into the
Pacific beyond the Golden Gate, just as John C. Fremont and
Joaquin Miller had watched and described it.

"What a place to set up some nets," exclaimed one of the
local bird-banding enthusiasts. "We could catch them as they come
over the hilltop between those pines."

This was a rare chance to catch quite a few winter migrants
and learn something about their travels. Permission was granted by
the park administration, and a few weeks later I reached the hilltop in late afternoon just as a half dozen young birdbanders were
setting up Japanese mist nets under the critical eyes of Howard
Cogswell and Richard Meweldt, professors of ornithology at nearby college campuses.

The East Bay Christmas Count, taken a few days earlier, had
included the Robin Roost where an estimate reached twenty
thousand birds! How many of them could they expect to catch
in these fragile nets which reached up only fifteen feet and
stretched forty or fifty feet across the hilltop?

The first answer came shortly after four o'clock when an
advance squad of robins came darting over the hill and collided
with the net. Banders John Ralph and Rich Stallcup rushed from
their ambush under the pines and began to free them from the
nets.

These first captures were hustled back to the ambush site and
bands placed on them. A college girl carefully entered each number in the notebook. Another student was shown by the professor
how to blow gently on the body plumage to expose the skin. The
amount of fat on the body of a migrant bird indicates how fast

74

and how far it has traveled, just as you would check your mileage speedometer to determine the length of the trip you took.

"Swish—whump—" More robins in the nets. There's one that got its tongue caught in the fine strands. Careful, it looks bad, but you can almost always disentangle a tongue without injury to the bird.

And so the roundup proceeded that afternoon until after sunset when a few latecomers were still getting into the nets. Close to three score birds had been captured, banded, and freed. The following years would reveal how far they would carry those metal identification anklets, and some were found in Oregon, Washington, and British Columbia.

During the next two years, the netters and banders returned many times to Joaquin Miller's hilltop. Some of the Palos Colorados robins participated in the rooftop experiment station at the State University of California at San Jose, where they were installed in open cages with perches wired to a master control panel. Their nightly movements as the overhead celestial pattern changed with the seasons helped to confirm the theory that birds set their migration courses by the stars.

Debut of the Barrow's goldeneye duck

The great robin phenomenon of Palos Colorados Canyon has made news stories and feature pages in the local press and on television, but in ornithological circles, it was far outranked by the sudden "adoption" of Lake Merritt as a winter home by the once-rare Barrow's goldeneye duck. I must admit to some puzzlement— even chagrin—over this sense of values held by my birder friends and associates. I grant that it *is* thrilling and rewarding to discover and to welcome a once-rare bird into your midst, but I still feel that such strange and inexplicable behavior as this homing instinct that produces the Robin Roost is of even greater nature and human interest. My media-friends and thousands of ordinary nature lovers feel the same, but not always the typical, dedicated birder, or "lifelister."

That is precisely why the three Barrow's goldeneyes that splashed down on Lake Merritt several years ago caused such a sensation in birding circles. Most local birders, including those near-fanatic lifelisters, had for years canvassed the bays and estuaries along the coast looking for this rare cousin of the common goldeneye duck.

Many had never quite caught up with Barrow's who wears a white crescent on his iridescent head instead of the roundish spot of the common goldeneye.

A handsome male Barrow's attended by two plain hens discovered Lake Merritt and liked it. Mornings, the trio would forage by diving all over the one hundred and fifty acres of lake and by afternoon, if the pleasure boats appeared, would settle on sheltered waters, surrounded by common goldeneyes and ruddy ducks.

This didn't make a news story in the press. It wasn't necessary. The word got around in birding circles. Birders of all degrees, ages, and conditions beat paths to Lakeside Park. Some we hadn't seen for years. Some had regarded birding at Lake Merritt as only for beginners.

Groups of these superior birders appeared at the office door, binoculars and telescopes at the ready. Or a taxi would disgorge a birder from another city who had headed directly for Lake Merritt from the airport or the hotel. It might be a doctor, sales manager, or educator who was expected at a convention in Oakland or San Francisco, but the prospect of adding a Barrow's goldeneye to a lifelist came first.

As park naturalists it was gratifying to share the spotlight by dropping everything and accompanying these visiting birders to the place along the shore where Mister Barrows and party could be pointed out. Some of the birder's excitement was bound to rub off on all present.

One of these lifelister Barrow's chasers was Bill. He had grown up in the Bay Area and become one of the sharpest birders. Then we lost him as he went away to attend a college of his choice in another city.

During that first winter season of the Era of the Barrow's, Bill, looking wan and haggard and tenderly supported by his mother, stood in the office doorway. He had just been released from the hospital after an appendectomy when word of Barrow's, a new bird for his lifelist, reached him.

We told Bill to look for the Barrow's from several points along the lake shore on this cold winter morning. His mother became concerned and insisted he would have to give up and return to her car. But it was obvious that Bill wouldn't accept such defeat. Grabbing his binoculars, he announced he'd walk along shore until he sighted Barrow's, operation be damned! We last saw him disappearing down the walk with mother trying to button up his overcoat and wrap a scarf around his neck. We heard later that he had found Barrow's, a precious new name for his growing lifelist.

The water birds of Lake Merritt and much of the aquatic estuarine life are inextricably related by a tidal canal to the shoreline and waters of Alameda like the heart to the aorta. When disease or foreign matter enters this circulatory system, the results are chaotic—as when sewage enters the lake or oil is dumped into the estuary. Some veteran lake-watchers still blame Alameda for filling its South Shore tideflats and discouraging the masses of pintails that commuted from there to Lake Merritt. Nevertheless, we permitted our surplus Canada geese to move to Alameda, where they animate the golf course, sometimes nest in private yards facing the lagoon, and in general enhance public relations, at least with bird lovers. In turn, the Greater and Snowy egrets, since adopting the Duck Islands as nesting sites in the spring of 1975, have depended more than ever on the goodies foraged along Alameda's shores.

Birds of the Alameda South Shore

The South Shore fill for upper-class housing and shopping, to our surprise and some embarrassment, has also developed new tideflats, beaches, and one beautiful salt marsh reserved by the East Bay Regional Park District "for the birds." Here the bird watchers and serious birders like the semimonthly census team are enjoying a heyday of observations. Shorebirds by the thousands, aptly called "the living sands of San Francisco Bay" by bird photographer Laurel Reynolds, haunt this shoreline from early fall into spring. Most of these species, from giant curlew to little wisps like the sandpipers, take off for the far north by May for their nesting cycle. Amazingly, many are back at Alameda by late July.

Here the birders themselves are on stage for the passing parade of curious folk and the apartment dwellers who peer at the scene below. Joggers, dog-walkers, delivery people stop to ascertain what we're doing, and apartment house tenants, sometimes clad in pajamas and dressing gowns, saunter over to interview us. What an opportunity to interest neophytes in birding! Occasionally one of these picture-window or balcony beach watchers does decide to join us, or at least to purchase an

Audubon Society membership and then to read more about the
Audubon cause.

When a pair of killdeer, the ubiquitous, garrulous year round
resident plover, decides to set up housekeeping on the gravel roof
of an apartment house, the entire neighborhood may get involved.
Everyone awaits with trepidation the day when their spindly precocious offspring must take the two-story jump to the ground
below and cross the busy street.

Now and then a Clapper rail, a coveted endangered species,
will emerge from the marsh during an extra high tide, walk calmly
up the beach and across the street, and then disappear into denser
landscaping to sit out the tide. Sometimes a platoon of magnificent
white pelicans from the South Bay wheels overhead and captures
the attention of the bayside dwellers. Only a flight of spaceships
or UFO's could attract more comment.

Across the shrinking Bay Farm Island Channel lies a battle
ground now being transformed into the Harbor Bay Isles residential
project. This vast tract was once the beautiful McCartney Marsh,
important feeding grounds for shorebirds, herons and ducks, a
spawning place for bay fish, and a mecca for marsh students and
birders. Then in the early 1960's private developers, backed by international financiers, cast lustful eyes upon it, and the battle was on.

The "bird women" of Alameda

Enter Junea W. Kelly, famed leader of the University's "Six
Trips Afield" and a longtime Alameda resident and shorebird
devotee. Junea had unsuccessfully resisted every step of the gigantic South Shore fill and development. She organized a new strike
force and sent them into the fray against the developers and ambitious city fathers who favored this project. Birders, environmentalists—even sportsmen—from far and near rallied to the cause.
Governmental agencies from Sacramento to Washington sent
spokesmen or pronouncements against this project. But the developers and local politicians, with their glib promises of greater
prosperity for Alameda, were too well organized and financed.
Finally McCartney Marsh was drained and filled with mud dredged
from offshore. This defeat was a crushing blow to Junea in the
twilight of her career.

Then came the Battle of San Leandro Bay, the large, shallow
body of water lying between Bay Farm Island and East Oakland.

Although long ago declared a State Game Refuge, this designation was only intended to discourage hunters and poachers. The Port of Oakland had long since filled most of the bordering marshy areas for industry and airport-related business. By 1972, the Port had already diked off and was preparing to fill the last remaining sizeable marsh tract in the Bay. This was the two hundred acre area now sadly dubbed the "Erstwhile Marsh," a vital feeding place for waterfowl and shorebirds and nesting site of stilts, rails, grebes, and ducks. The next objective was Doolittle Pond, a fifteen-acre diked pond whose borders and tiny islands at high tide offer shelter to an incredible, jam-packed mass of shorebirds. It can be an eye stopper for alert or curious motorists on busy Doolittle Drive which runs between the Old Airport and San Leandro Bay.

Now a second "Bird Woman of Alameda," Mrs. Elsie Roemer, a longtime admirer and pupil of Junea Kelly, represented the task forces who would engage the Port of Oakland and other political and business interests who preferred business to birds around the Bay. A powerful new force, the San Francisco Bay Conservation and Development Commission (BCDC) could, by this time, forbid or approve bayshore development, and to our surprise the United States Army Corps of Engineers, an old foe of environmentalists, also came over to the side of the Bay- and bird-savers. No, Doolittle Pond could *NOT* be filled with garbage or solid waste ruled the Engineers. Under a BCDC grandfather clause, Erstwhile Marsh must be ceded to industry, but the long strip of Arrowhead Marsh extending far into the Bay was set aside for the birds.

"Who would protect Doolittle Pond and the remaining marsh strips, and who would provide access to fishing and recreation on San Leandro Bay?" the Port commissioners now inquired. At this crucial stage, the East Bay Regional Park District stepped in. With an acceptable lease and some State and Federal openspace and conservation funds, they would add this area to their far-flung empire. Pushed by a growing citizen force, the good commissioners agreed to this, and we will soon enjoy a San Leandro Bay Shoreline Park.

These years of struggle, council and commission hearings, hours in the field convincing various officials of the values of marsh and wildlife, stubborn resistance and attacks by some politicians and developers, took their toll of Elsie. She was obliged to retire to a less active role, but she had a worthy successor to push

79

into the breech. A much younger woman, Leora Feeny, the third "Bird Woman," had followed Elsie and had made her own mark locally by writing a brilliant series on the Alameda shore birds for the Alameda Times Star. The torch was handed to Leora and she bravely accepted it.

Another crisis was looming in the spring of 1977. The developers of Harbor Bay Isles on the McCartney Marsh site had decided they didn't want to dedicate the one hundred foot peripheral shoreline strip promised the birders and fishermen. After a few encounters with Leora and her reorganized forces, they changed their minds. This time city hall even sided with the birders!

Another victory was chalked up, but this doesn't mean that henceforth the remaining marshes and shorelines of Alameda or of San Francisco Bay are completely secure for fish and wildlife and for citizens who love these natural endowments. There must be more Juneas, Elsies, and Leoras to carry on future encounters.

These accounts have dealt with some of the more spectacular activities of birds and birders. The exciting field trips, the lively competition of the lifelisters who aspire to see *all* the species in their state or country, the patient nest watchers or blind-sitting photographers—all these represent the many phases of one of the fastest-growing hobbies in America today.

Binocular and camera pointers already far outnumber shotgun and rifle users on the public lands of North America and may soon exceed all the fishing poles and rods as well. Just consider the shift of impact on America Outdoors! No costly fish hatcheries or planting programs, no pheasant farms or posted, patrolled hunting clubs are required by these millions of bird watchers and related nature watchers. All they ask is that adequate countryside and habitat be left alone, unspoiled, unpolluted. Even the familiar "keep out" signs shouldn't be meant for them, they feel, as they have never shot a farmer's cow nor littered a stream bank (at least, I hope not).

"Will your nature lovers fight to save some of these places from reckless development or pollution?" your equally dedicated fisherman or nimrod may demand. After all, it has been mainly the monies raised from licenses and taxes on ammunition and equipment which has provided and maintained the many state and federal wildlife refuges and "game management areas" so heavily patronized by the bird watching fraternity. These far outrank in acreage all the tracts bought or maintained by Audubon and other protective groups.

Yes, this new generation of bird and nature lovers will fight. They will fight the proposed highway, subdivision, or dam site all the way up to the steps of state capitols and Congress. They will lay aside their binoculars, cameras, and notebooks to march together in a common cause. Their sons and daughters will be seen carrying picket signs in front of the contractor who would fill and build over a particular marsh, meadow, or stream; rescuing and cleaning oiled birds; or manning sidewalk tables with petitions to save some natural scenery or wildlife resource.

This growing movement which has united so many different kinds of outdoor users and nature lovers in a common front against despoilers and polluters may ultimately mean the salvation of our scenic and natural resources—provided, of course, that the world's population can be stabilized in the near future.

Man Tries Bird Management:
Some Successes and Some Failures

What happens to that pintail or scaup duck you feed on the park lake all winter and which suddenly is gone one April day? Or the Canada geese that stop briefly and call from a marsh a few days in October and again in April? Where do they finally stop to make their nests and rear their little broods?

The answers to your questions, and many more like them, are readily available due to an active bird banding program. Since the era of World War One, these dedicated, painstaking banding operations provided the only reliable records of bird travels, longevity, and sex ratios, until the more recent advent of plastic markers, distinctive plumage dyes, and bio-telemetry (radio collars).

Although an Oakland legend and a function religiously carried on for some decades, the annual roundup and banding of the Lake Merritt ducks hadn't impressed certain city fathers and politicos of its real value to the city. A considerable amount of gardener and laborer time was spent on this project. In fact, the mayor who took office soon after Park Superintendent William Penn Mott's arrival hadn't been sold on several of Mott's progressive and costly ideas, like a park naturalist and a Science Center in the park. Mayors often influence or control city councils, and councilmen decide whether or not department heads get the wherewithal to develop their innovative programs. Obviously, Mr. Mott and his followers needed to win over His Honor.

The breakthrough came where least expected. It didn't take a tactful intermediary nor a professional public relations person. It was all due to a single migrant pintail duck that lost its way, much like the celebrated "Wrongway Corrigan" of aviation history.

Thousands of pintails banded at Lake Merritt from 1926 to 1953 had followed the Pacific or Central (Rocky Mountain) flyways during their subsequent migrations. If some had wandered to other flyways, they died undiscovered and unreported. Then one day during the 1955 hunting season an envelope was delivered from the United States Fish and Wildlife Service that was to change migration history for the Lake Merritt ducks. A male pintail banded at the lake in November of 1953 had been shot at Anabyr, Siberia in September 1954! The Soviet wildlife authorities had dutifully returned the band to Washington. It wasn't the first California banded duck to cross the Bering Straits to Siberia, but it was all ours to claim.

Superintendent Mott recognized the potentials of this incident, and quickly carried the news to city hall. The effect of this international recognition of Oakland on the mayor and certain councilmen was miraculous. The mayor did a complete turnaround in support of the park department. Superintendent Mott, the naturalist program, and all the "bird nuts" suddenly came into their own at city hall. We had scored a diplomatic breakthrough of the Iron Curtain. Our "lucky duck" and a few others like it might even lead to better relations between the peoples of California and the Soviet Union.

Bands such as the one worn by the "international courier" duck have identified Lake Merritt birds since the late 1920's. In those days right through the 1940's, the annual duck banding roundups were top social as well as scientific events. I sometimes wonder now how those hundreds of pintails and widgeons were banded and properly recorded in the U.S. Biological Survey schedules and files.

Mr. E.W. Ehman, a successful businessman and ardent waterfowl hunter, offered his services as "cooperator" with the

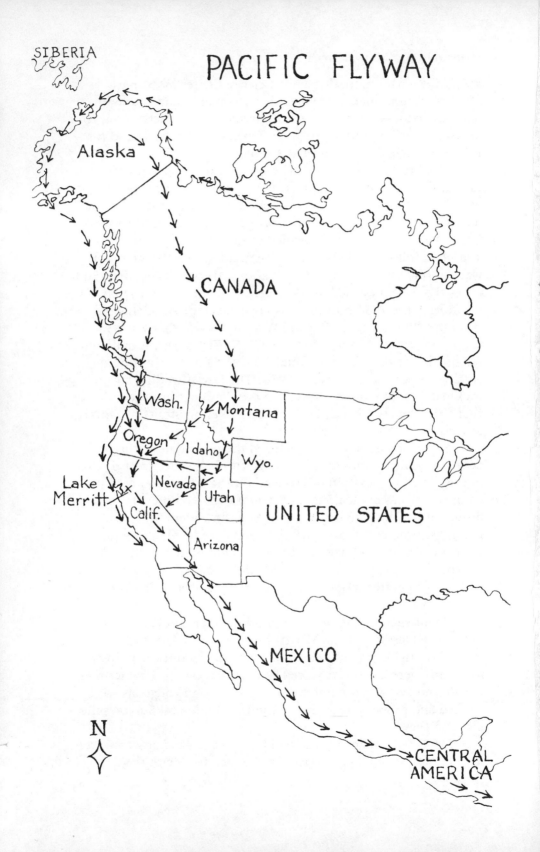

Biological Survey for the purpose of banding the migrant ducks at Lake Merritt. Ehman believed, as did many sportsmen and ornithologists, that these winter visitors were spending their summers on the prairies of western Canada and even beyond. Regular mass banding, records of return migrants to Lake Merritt, and reports of gunned birds and pickups would do much to confirm the theory.

Officials of the Biological Survey accepted the offer and promised to issue as many bands as Ehman could use. He, at his personal expense, promised to furnish adequate facilities and help to band the birds and to maintain accurate records. The Oakland Park Department agreed to host Ehman's duck banders, to set up the big trap in the Duck Pond enclosure, and to bait and help catch the birds.

Everybody helped

Mr. Ehman, a dedicated and generous man, went overboard in staging his banding roundups. Early in the morning of each annual banding day, he arrived with a truck loaded with tables, folding chairs, tarpaulins if rainy, and workmen to handle all the paraphernalia. Sandwiches and tanks of hot coffee were delivered later by his chauffeur and secretary. There was always more than enough for all the helpers. And the volunteer helpers. They included Mr. Ehman's secretary, his son and other family members, several duck-hunting or social associates, and a number of newspaper reporters and photographers. A few Boy Scouts and one or two amateur ornithologists usually joined the crew, and sometimes a visiting professional dropped in.

In spite of all the showy display, this was not primarily a big social affair. There were sometimes a thousand pintails, several hundred widgeons, and hundreds of mud hens trapped when the gates of the big wireframe trap dropped. Feathers and squawks filled the air. Only then could the tables and chairs be hastily set up and the swarm of helpers admitted to the scene.

Notwithstanding the blunders and nuisances committed by amateurs, and the interruptions to pose for the press, all the trapped birds were brought to the tables for inspection. New migrants received aluminum leg bands while returned birds were carefully recorded and reported.

There were comparatively few mallard residents at the Lake in the 1930's, and they were usually passed up as non-migrants.

85

Baiting-in migrant ducks for banding. Original Duck Island shows in background of this photo, about 1950.

Two banded pintails set free by Park Naturalist Covel.

The Pekins and hybrid types went to county institution mess halls. The pigeons were distributed to any helpers who wanted them. In those days, every public institution had kitchen help who could clean and dress ducks, and every family had some use for pigeons.

In 1940, Mr. Ehman painstakingly constructed a master chart with colored pins to indicate the travels of the Lake Merritt pintails, widgeons, and mud hens. Even the scorned, weak-winged mud hen won a few colors on this map.

The great experiment of Lake Merritt duck banding paid off handsomely. Hundreds of pintails and widgeons were found in the western Canadian provinces, the Yukon, across Alaska, and up to the Bering Sea. The bands removed from individuals which died from various causes were returned to the Biological Survey at Washington, and Mr. Ehman and the Oakland Park Department received a constrant stream of forms telling them of the birds' history. As a result of these records, school children, bird lovers, nimrods, chambers of commerce, newspaper reporters, and feature writers across the United States and Canada heard about Lake Merritt and the migrant ducks.

The unlimited construction era of post-World War Two brought devastation to the bird feeding areas on the shores of San Francisco Bay. Several thousand pintails that commuted nightly from Lake Merritt to these ancestral feeding grounds found instead land fills for commerce, airports, and new housing. Grain feedings and other handouts received at the Park were not enough to support such a large pintail flock. By the 1950's their numbers began to diminish until the fall-winter season of 1968-69 when we counted fewer than twenty-five. The widgeons still came because they loved the lawn grass, but now busier thoroughfares, more dog walkers, joggers, and high-rise apartments finally reduced the widgeon population to a few individuals. It became imperative that we find another duck population to band.

During the years of the great pintail roundups, over one thousand canvasbacks, hundreds of scaups or bluebills, and other diving-duck species in smaller lots had roomed and boarded on the Lake Merritt Waterfowl Refuge without paying their just dues to science. They accepted grain and other handouts along the shore and commuted to San Francisco Bay for the night. But not one ever ventured ashore to submit to capture and banding. These cagey divers had to be sampled.

David Farrow, Jr., then the assistant naturalist, helped me in experiments with various deepwater traps, built close to shore and operated by pull-string mechanisms. We were pleased and proud when we began catching canvasback and scaup to place identification rings on their legs. This was a "first" in the history of the Refuge. These species, too, turned up in western Canada and Alaska but didn't return for retrapping in the following years in the same ratio as the pintail and widgeon.

The entertainment and educational values of these offshore traps were considerable, but the human interference and operational difficulties were frustrating. Water levels of the lake are controlled by flood gates. During the winter rains, the lake is kept very low to prevent overflow so the shy diving ducks avoided the traps when they had to drag bottom. This was solved by building a trap in the middle of the lake where there would be a minimum of eighteen to twenty-four inches of water at all times. However, the water level would reach a maximum of three or four feet so the operator needed chest-high waders, and even then sometimes scooped up cold water when netting the evasive quarry. A short funnel opening just below the surface allowed divers only to enter this trap which was baited with grain inside and out.

This is how we gradually became one of the principal, early diving-duck banding operations on the Pacific Flyway. It has been fortunate that four assistant naturalists in turn have been able and willing to row out to this trap daily to scoop out the catch. As one man said, "It's all in a day's work."

Wild bird-banding is not for sport and thrills

Any park naturalist program that includes bird banding enjoys a magnetic attraction to bird lovers—even to those who wouldn't carry binoculars along a windy beach or a forest trail. The idea of trapping and banding wild birds catches the fancy of many bird students and observers, and they would gladly try their luck if it were that simple. But it isn't, and professional naturalists and banders have to dissuade many would-be banders from applying for permits. Have you ever tried to identify one of those many species of American warblers in fall plumage, particularly a young of the year? If you can't, you better not apply for a banding permit. If your bird is recognized later by some fellow bander as another species, you're in trouble. Most neophyte

Assistant Naturalist David Farrow, Jr., scoops up male canvasback in deepwater banding trap. Mallards were unwanted.

David Farrow, Jr., prepares to band a male scaup duck at deepwater trap. Mud hens were uninvited at this trap.

banders work under the supervision of a veteran bander who holds
the master permit because the Banding Office of the Fish and Wildlife Service insists on meticulous records.

Wild bird-banding is not intended to furnish sport and thrills
to curious bird lovers. It is a serious, scientific pursuit. The U.S.
Fish and Wildlife Service, successor to the U.S. Biological Survey,
which issues the bird bands and keeps the master records of all
banded North American birds, insists that banders have specific
projects. Applicants for banding permits must be at least eighteen
and must be vouched for by three well-known ornithologists.

For many years bands issued by the U.S. Fish and Wildlife
Service bore the legend: "Avise/write Fish & Wildlife Service,
Washington, D.C." *Avise* meant "notify" to French Canadians
and to Latin Americans. On the smaller bands, the abbreviations
for the Service read: "F&W Serv" or initials equally puzzling to
the uninitiated. Small wonder that finders mailed bands to various
nonexistent addresses in Washington—even on occasion to the
"Foul Water Service"! Then someone came up with the address
"Bird Band." What a welcome suggestion. "Bird Band" as an
address was unmistakable in the English-speaking world. All new
bands (even a hummingbird band, size 0) will bear these words:
"Avise, Bird Band, Wash DC USA."

Bird banding correspondence, interest aroused by distant
recoveries of birds, and bird observations make for better understanding between countries. Migrant birds know no international
boundaries, and according to the visionaries, neither will man in
that Utopia of the future.

Now what about some other kinds of bands or markers that
you may have seen birds wearing? Various illegitimate adornments
are unintentionally picked up by diving ducks which must find
food in the mud where much of the litter of city drains flows.
Colored elastic bands are frequently worn around the necks and
between the mandibles of the bill by many of the Lake Merritt
canvasbacks, scaups, and ruddies. Some come wearing the plastic
frames which encase six-packs, and one canvasback arrived with
a pair of spectacle frames around its neck.

Such handicapped ducks are indeed lucky if they subsequent-
ly blunder into a bander's water trap as they often do at Lake
Merritt where they are relieved of their troublesome "chokers."
We have also removed many a small fish hook from a duck's tongue

90

and bill. Lead shot in the digestive tract picked up during foraging on shooting ponds is another major cause of duck mortality. Wildlife management authorities have tried for years to have iron or alloy shot pellets legally replace the noxious lead pellets. This may soon become federal law on all the flyways.

Too many suitors

When does polygamy pay off in waterfowl management? Mallards became a serious problem around the Duck Feeding area of Lakeside Park in the early 1950's due to too-successful production and nursery care of the ducklings. When pintails began to return in August and September, there were a thousand or more new-generation mallards dominating the feeding pool and even the pedestrian walks to such an extent that passage was difficult. At the beach-feeding station, they literally covered the shallow water area and threatened to take over.

The fecundity and zeal of the resident mallards eventually forced us into another phase of management. Promiscuity is the rule among most male ducks, and at city lakes like Lake Merritt, they find it easy to practice with utter abandon. Lack of individual territories and natural hiding places for the hens when they leave their incubating duties or bring their broods ashore exposes them to the amorous passions of the idle drakes.

Scenes of mass rape become common. Normal pursuit and mating you can usually explain to the onlookers, but this near-drowning and mutilation of the passive hens evokes expressions of horror and shock. Passionate drakes may even line up to wait their turns! Occasionally the ducklings with the mother become confused and eventually are lost in all the excitement. Enforced polygamy maintains a happier situation for such a mallard colony so each fall we held drake roundups in the feeding area.

The first mallard roundups staged for the express purpose of separating and exporting the troublesome drakes attracted some bystander interest and a few suspicious queries. This was plainly not a banding operation. We'd discovered years before that mallard banding didn't pay off because park-reared birds refused to join the wild migrants.

We simply had to tell the citizens who asked that these handsome birds were being exported to marshes north of San Francisco Bay as a duck management operation. Yes, they would have to

Hatching day in a mallard nest; note "egg-tooth" on bill of just-pipped duckling.

Julie and a hatful of duck-lings bound for Duckling Nursery.

92

take their chances with the hunters within a few weeks. Yes, some might fly back to Lake Merritt, but we hoped not many. Well, Ma'am would you rather see half our mallard hens raped to death and their ducklings lost to the gulls next spring?

While answering such questions and parrying others, the arrival of the Department of Fish and Game vehicle with its emblazoned emblem and uniformed game agents assured dubious bystanders that we told the truth. Pretty soon one or two crates of baffled protesting greenheads were off for those marshes. If the numerous mallard hens left behind suffered any profound emotional shock, we never detected it!

With the cooperation of local fish and game or wildlife conservation agents, this is one possible solution for public duck pond managers or concerned citizens. The many tame muscovies, Chinese Pekins, and hybrids you may dispose of according to custom and local ordinances. But beware of sending any normal, free-flying mallards, no matter how tame, to the nearest welfare kitchen. Your state wildlife agents or the Feds will take a dim view of such liberties and may even threaten to ship *you* "up the river" to some place with free room and board.

The American coot or mud hen is a remarkable waterfowl. This ubiquitous cousin of the rails and cranes actually associates with ducks in fall and winter, motivated more by convenience and rewards than by preference for their company. The coot is adaptable to a high degree and gregarious except during its nesting season. Nature, or the process of evolution, has given it fringed toes to swim and dive better than its relatives, the rails and gallinules. It can also forage easily on land when it becomes essential to reach an abundant food supply. Lawn grass and other soft vegetation are top choices.

Migrant coots begin to appear at Lake Merritt in September. Nobody sees them dropping in like the duck migrants. As if ashamed of their awkward, labored flight, they choose to arrive in the darkness. Then one morning several new coots are being challenged by the one or two pairs that stayed over the summer. By late October there may be several hundred—even a thousand or more. In spring they are also reluctant to take leave from this free and secure board and lodging, and many will linger well into April.

How far do these fringe-toed fowl with the lagging flight really fly when they must do so? As a rule, no farther than necessary to reach a hospitable pond or slough in the back country. For many years they have been trapped and banded at Lake Merritt, at the cost of vicious bill digs at the handlers' exposed skin. Comparatively few coot bands have been returned from areas beyond the Sacramento-San Joaquin Delta and the Great Valley of California, but some band-wearers did make it to Oregon and Washington, and at least a couple flew over the border into Canada. Study of the coot is a neglected research area, and ornithologists still have much to learn about this humble fowl.

Coots and golf don't mix

A community that builds a golf course adjacent to a marsh or designs a pond into its new course doesn't realize that it actually creates an outdoor dining room for coots. They present a more serious problem in California because most Pacific coast waterfowl shooters look with disdain on the lowly coot and its flesh.

Every fall and winter, the Lake Merritt naturalists received telephone calls from harassed golf course managers around San Francisco Bay. These unhappy officials were caught between fires of the irate golfers, who dislike walking over coot manure, and their local bird lovers who don't play golf but do admire the coots on the greens and even come to feed them when they retreat to the nearest water.

A typical conversation went like this. "We've got a problem down here with these damn coots on our golf course. How many coots do you have at Lake Merritt and how do you keep them off your lawns?"

"Well, we average between six and eight hundred coots every winter. They all feed on our lawns together with approximately one hundred and fifty geese, but we've got over a hundred acres in lawns around the lake."

"What the hell, don't people complain about all the coot — — — — when they walk or sit down?"

"No, not very often," we explained. "Coots are only here in the fall and winter and most of our visitors are bird lovers and bird feeders. We've trained the coots to stay off our bowling and putting greens." (A slight exaggeration as there are fences around the bowling greens and the small putting green is too hard-packed and close-cropped for the coots.)

94

"That may be all right with you guys," said our caller, plainly warming up a bit. "It's my neck down here. When we couldn't run the coots off with dogs or blank shells, I let the police department come in during the early morning hours and shoot them. Now I've got that Audubon outfit after us. They threaten to picket our next council meeting. There just has to be some way to discourage these damn birds."

"You might try building a high fence between your duck pond and the greens," I suggested. "Coots are poor flyers, and they would hesitate to get cornered before they could get up and over a fence."

"No, no, that wouldn't work. Our architect would never go for that—and besides, we couldn't find the money to build one."

I remembered one last resort for these coot-plagued greens. Falcons. Peregrine and prairie falcons flown by their owners and trainers have performed brilliantly in chasing coots off several northern California golf courses.

"How about getting a falconer to fly his bird over your greens," I suggested. "Next to shotguns with live ammunition,

coots are mortally afraid of hawks and falcons. Why don't you give it a try?"

"Oh, we tried that," he said, "but it wound up with the falconer losing his bird. He had to let it eat a coot now and then. His falcon must have eaten a sick bird because it suddenly died. Now we can't get another falconer to risk his bird."

I'm forced to admit I didn't have an answer for that contingency. It would be difficult to get enough insurance to cover a working falcon against the chance of contracting a disease from his victims. Like the owner of a well-trained retriever, the professional falconer might refuse any price for his bird.

Meanwhile, the omnipresent coots in small armies go marching and munching across California pastures, grain fields, park lawns, and golf greens. Hunters are encouraged to shoot and eat more "whitebills" which really yield delicious dark meat when properly prepared. Some years the coot season is extended many weeks after the close of other waterfowl shooting. Duck and goose populations may fluctuate alarmingly, but the coot holds its own despite many handicaps and enemies.

Confessions of a bird lover

Others too have had their moments of concern in this area of bird management. A well-known local ornithologist was perturbed as he told me this story—a sort of confession that would certainly ruin his image with a lot of bird lovers, and he didn't want that to happen.

It all started with the familiar problem of birds versus airplanes. Hordes of gulls flew en masse from the San Leandro garbage dump right next to the Oakland International Airport. Somebody had estimated the winter gull population to number as much as thirty thousand, and sooner or later there was sure to be a jet collision.

The local ornithologist was called in as a professional advisor. He and a few other dedicated bird watchers like Mrs. Elsie Roemer, the "Bird Woman of Alameda," were given special permission to drive on the outer perimeter roads of the vast bay-fill airport to "follow the birds." Thousands of shore birds and many waterfowl had been displaced when this vast fill was placed over their ancestral tideland feeding grounds. But at low tide they still fed along the tideland fringe beyond the airport dikes, and at high tide, they moved over on the open lands beyond the runways to enjoy relative security for their loafing periods. Sometimes the smaller shorebirds rose up in clouds to worry pilots taking off or landing, but this threat was minor compared to that presented by the gulls just across the slough around the garbage dumps.

The airport management learned that an oil company had developed experimentally a "gull control" chemical which they wanted to test on the West Coast. When mixed with sugar and bread crumbs to be eaten by the gulls, it produced weird contortions and squawks from the hapless birds. This was intended to scare off the other gulls.

The ornithologist agreed to represent the gulls' interests, if not the bird lovers', at the first trial of these "goof balls." He met the oil company chemists and airport officials at the garbage dump where they proceeded to strew the bait. Gulls being gulls, a few took the bait. Soon signs of malaise began to appear among the birds which had partaken of the fare. They twisted their heads and necks into strange shapes and tried to vomit—an operation that comes easily for a gull. Somewhat shakily they spread their wings and got into the air where the wind from the southeast picked them up, and away they went off toward the city of Alameda. This wasn't exactly in the plan, as the afflicted birds were supposed to remain in the feeding area to warn off the others.

Some of the stricken gulls, still lurching drunkenly and screaming in the worst gull language, landed in the streets and on the lawns in Alameda. Startled citizens telephoned the police department, city hall, and the Humane Society. The local press heard about it, but fortunately didn't make a big story out of it.

The ornithologist, the airport managers, and chemical company officials retreated from the field of operations to hold a strategy conference well out of reach of the press and investigators. Discovery and publicity at this stage would jeopardize the whole experiment.

A few days later, the team went back to the garbage dumps with dosages of the chemical and the proper sugar and bread formula. This time it worked better. If some of the victims got into the air, they never reached a city street to alert the bird lovers. And whatever they screamed as they felt the effects of the "goof balls" really did alarm and scare off many other gull diners at the dumps.

Six months later, a story in the leading metropolitan newspaper broke the news to the public. The Port of Oakland announced that use of this chemical over a five-month period had reduced the dump and runway gull population from an estimated thirty thousand to about three hundred. There never was any concerted protest over this *fait accompli.* In fact the airport stated its intention to continue using this new product during the next winter season.

The Shutter Bug

Any zoo, museum, or nature center director who doesn't establish close relations with the local papers, television and radio stations may not survive very long in his chosen career nowadays.

We have always gone all out to help the gentlemen of the press and other news media when they have come to us for a story. Sometimes they showed up with scratch pads and cameras for a story that was no longer there. The editor or studio program director conceived a newsworthy story on the waterfowl at the right time, but some hotter news broke and the birds had to wait. The trouble was—winter migrant ducks wouldn't extend their stay for a write-up, nor would the Canada geese delay their mating or hatching until the camera crew could make it.

Two television photographers came one day in late winter to take footage of the trapping and banding of the diving ducks. By this date most of the canvasbacks and scaup had left for their northern breeding grounds, and we were about to close the trapping operation until the next fall. But the television fellows couldn't wait until next fall; they had been sent out on an important assignment. We told them to return in two days, and we would try to have some subjects for banding shots.

It developed that not another canvasback or scaup would enter the water trap. In desperation we rounded up some mud hens, hoping we might substitute them for diving ducks in the lake trap.

But when the cameramen returned, they wouldn't go for it. Diving ducks they had to have.

There was only one recourse to bail us out of a jam and keep our image for their station. With misgivings I told Assistant Naturalist Farrow to take the canvasback drake and two hens out of the display cage and use them as models. They were being held for shipment to an eastern zoo. They would be banded for the camera and then unbanded and returned to their temporary home.

Dave and the wildlife shooters took off for the deepwater trap, men and cameras bogging down the little skiff almost to the gunwales. The canvasbacks were in one gunny sack and in another were a few mud hens to be used for "crowd effects."

The photographers took agonizing pains with their setup at the trap. I knew those poor canvasbacks would get waterlogged and exhausted if they ran them through too many rehearsals or repeat performances. Dave could take it because earlier in the season he frequently worked out there as long as two hours netting birds and banding and recording each one.

The expedition returned. The canvasbacks had survived, but they were three tired, bedraggled ducks. I guess it was quite obvious that I wasn't so much concerned for the health of the cameramen who had worked out of their element.

Tiger hunting in Oakland

Emil, an avid photographer, was retired from the business world and from more active sports. He took up photography as a challenging hobby without the physical exertions he had been warned to forego. But somewhere along the way, photography took over Emil.

"Picture of the Month," "Nature Picture of the Year," and other coveted and elusive prizes became the guiding goals and motivations of Emil's life. Just as sure as booze dominates some men's lives, so did this prize-picture obsession dominate Emil's waking hours. It was even capable of transforming this ordinarily friendly man into a demanding perfectionist who would sweep aside all obstacles to achieve *the picture.* At such times his heavy foreign accent and insistent manner combined to impress or even to terrify some humans who stood in his way. These unfortunates may even have been drafted as on-the-spot helpers in Emil's clever plot to circumvent obstacles and get *the picture.*

100

Emil was a good photographer—no mistake about that. And for those who helped, he always had beautiful color slides to share with them. Boys who worked with nature and collected small animals intrigued him. If they lent him a hand when he needed it, he responded with appreciation and generosity. But those moments of "lending Emil a hand" were often traumatic experiences for those boys.

Small reptiles and amphibians—the sort he could find in the park museums and in some boys' private home collections—became Emil's specialty for a brief period. Some of his close-ups of these subjects were really eye fillers. We've known some squeamish lady viewers to react with gasps of horror when his picture of a snake swallowing a white rat was flashed on a screen four feet high. And some of his intimate studies of hairy caterpillars chomping on leaf blades were terrific.

But Emil wasn't easily satisfied, even with those wildlife shots which were close to perfection. Take the case of the snakes at lunch. Those pictures revealed enough detail to flip a delicate stomach and send the viewer stumbling out of the hall for fresh air. Still there was something lacking in them for Emil. Blood! Now snakes swallow their lunch whole. No matter how bulky and

Wildlife photographers Roger Tory Peterson and Laurel Reynolds.

101

difficult the menu item, rarely does any blood show. But Emil could fix that. Just a matter of having someone find the right shade of nail polish and add it to the Kodachrome. Good try Emil, but some sharp eyes or snake expert detected this fakery. At least that is the story I got from one of Emil's young cooperators.

One day Emil stomped into the office looking even more perturbed than usual and displayed a sizeable rip in his trousers. Emil was really shaken as he related his story in disconnected pieces.

This started when Emil inquired about the chances of photographing the young tigers at Knowland Park Zoo. He spoke to the director and was off—loaded for tiger. At the zoo, Emil introduced himself and established his status as a wildlife photographer. This got him the special privilege of getting over the barrier and on the outer wall of the tigers' grotto, as far as anyone could safely venture. But this still didn't offer him the "intimate portraits" he really wanted. So he complained a bit about this and asked how he could move in closer.

The head keeper was not willing to sacrifice a man to those boisterous five-month-old tiger cubs—even for a good picture. But a young man standing by made Emil an irresistible offer.

"I've got a young tiger at home, and you can come and photograph it as much as you want because he is real tame," he said.

Emil got the name and address and was off on this fresh tiger scent. It led to a house in Piedmont, once the exclusive and wealthy community of the Eastbay.

The proprietor and a charming girl admitted Emil and his load of camera gear. Then all three walked through this spacious house which bore many visible marks of a large-animal habitat. They called for Simba, but Simba didn't respond until they had descended the back stairs to the garden and opened the basement door.

A big cat-like beast appeared and bounded straight at Emil. In fact, the animal proved so friendly that Emil could barely fend it off with his tripod.

"You could hardly tell whether it was friends or mad," Emil related. "My Gawd, it almost wrecked my camera. And see what it did to my leg!"

Then Simba gave a big leap and cleared the fence into the neighbor's yard. And from that yard to the next. So Emil was

102

enlisted to help round up the playful animal. This proved such a herculean effort that he quite forgot about getting more close-ups. In fact he didn't even notice this spotted yellow feline was really a lion cub instead of a tiger!

Emil's "tiger" suddenly broke into the news. It might have remained a rather open neighborhood secret for awhile longer if Simba's owner hadn't taken it for a walk in a public playground in Piedmont. Then startled observers got word to the police department who in reality had been tipped off some months before that they "had a lion in town."

City hall now was goaded to drastic action. Their chief of police reported in embarrassment that there wasn't any law specifically prohibiting the keeping of a lion. So the city council hurriedly adopted an emergency ordinance to that effect and told the chief to get on with his duty.

But Simba, a handsome eight-month-old lion cub, had already become a public figure. Children from all over Piedmont and a few outlying places trooped up to see "The Lion of Windsor Avenue." Quite a few grownups went too, and traffic suddenly became a problem on this once quiet street. The nearest elementary school sent a delegation to city hall with 232 pupils' names on a petition to "save Simba from a cage."

It was all very disconcerting to the chief of police, the honorable council, and the cause of law and order in Piedmont. At least one prominent attorney volunteered to defend the two owners of Simba, and the local S.P.C.A. was approached to determine if they could house Simba while the legal battle went on.

By the end of the week, Simba's masters had wearied of the fight. It was announced that Simba had been removed from Piedmont to another address in an unidentified city, and the case of the law collapsed for want of lions to prosecute. The chief said he would next ask the council to enact "a more exclusive law forbidding all zoo-type creatures, including tigers, boa constrictors, jaguars, cheetahs, and others." He recalled that Piedmont once "had a guy who used to ride around on a motorcycle with rattlesnakes under his cap." And he was right because I knew this gentleman, a Mr. Shaw, but the snake he carried under his cap had been defanged.

Shortly afterward, Emil called to ask if I had heard all the fuss about his "tiger" on Windsor Avenue. I said that I had — and reminded him that it was really a lion. I am still puzzled that this man who used to be a big game hunter hadn't distinguished between spots and stripes when first confronting his quarry.

The high jumping ducklings

Of all the waterfowl hatchings in public places and of all the battles to protect the broods—affairs where citizens aided parent mallards, geese, swans, and others—none ever attracted more attention on the Lake Merritt scene than the case of Juliet and her balcony broods.

Juliet, and in fact several other ingenious female associates of Juliet, discovered prize nesting sites in the flower boxes which decorated the second floor of the Sailboat House on the Lake. This was some years ago and in an era when we seemed to have more time to observe and record such vignettes of nature as this. The Sailboat House had a caretaker's quarters on the second floor, and this sympathetic fellow, Wally, served as a willing informant during the crucial days of the hatchings of the balcony nesters.

When Juliet the First was discovered sitting on her clutch of a dozen eggs, Wally summoned me. The big question was: should we try to catch the ducklings on hatching day or wait to see how they would make the descent of fourteen feet to the hard concrete dock below. I held out for the latter course in the interest of science. This choice brought some scathing comments from the emotional bird lovers who could only see a picture of squashed ducklings.

The big event began during an evening, and by the first rays of dawn, most of Juliet's brood were freed of their shells and wobbling dizzily across the flower box. What could a mother do? Romeo, now a disinterested father, was somewhere off with the other boys.

While we watched, Juliet flew down on the dock below, then into the water, and began calling her ducklings. Pretty soon we were somewhat surprised to see one of the babies step right off the rim of the flower box and sail downward until it hit the deck with a plop. Before we could run over to examine this one, another came plopping down, then a third—a fourth. Then there was a pause while the others held back. Juliet, quacking excitedly, left the water and walked over toward the fallen ones.

104

One by one the high jumpers recovered their senses, picked themselves up, and wobbled across the dock to join their mother. Juliet then returned to the water and called some more. Another jump of two feet was needed to launch the ducklings into the water. Here they heistated. It was as if too much was being demanded of them. Finally, they took the leap to join mother in the Lake. But she remained right there, calling the backward children still up on the balcony. After a few minutes, down came number five, then six, seven . . . eight . . . nine. Ten and eleven were cowards who refused to take the chance so we carried them down.

Juliet and her brood reached the Duck Pond later in the day and were gathered up and placed in the Mallard Nursery Apartments for security. But this was just the beginning of "the balcony nesters and the jumping ducklings."

A short time later Wally told us there was another mallard hen sitting on eggs under the nasturtiums in the flower box. This time I remembered the wildlife photographer, Mrs. Laurel Reynolds of Piedmont, who was in the process of making a Lake Merritt Waterfowl film for use in the naturalist program. Mrs. Reynolds had achieved nationwide recognition for her intimate bird portraits shown on the Audubon Wildlife Film Tours.

Like the professional she was, Mrs. Reynolds came down immediately to plan her camera setup for Hatching Day Two. She was shocked, like the other bird lovers, when she saw the height of the balcony boxes and the concrete landing strip. I assured her that the first jumpers all landed safely, if somewhat dazed. I even showed her the ducklings which were growing up rapidly in the nursery. Still, she didn't seem convinced.

On Hatching Day Two, Laurel Reynolds, who had remained "on call," was called, and she promised to be down within minutes. I guess I shouldn't have shown any surprise when Laurel asked for a hand getting her equipment from the car to the lower deck of the boathouse. It included a bulky air mattress completely inflated.

Laurel said she really didn't doubt that the first family had survived their rough landings, but she just didn't want to watch such a test of duckling resilience and fortitude, and besides, she was sure people in her film audiences would complain if she showed ducklings plopping on pavement. So, would I mind placing the mattress very carefully right where they would hit—if,

indeed, these ducklings were silly enough to jump like the first brood did.

This second nestful of mallards took their brave jumps for Laurel's movie camera. The episode became part of the film record of the normal and the eccentric behavior of the Lake Merritt waterfowl—and nobody saw the poor babes hit concrete, thanks to Laurel Reynolds.

In following years, Juliet and other balcony nesters have jumped their broods to the deck below without benefit of air mattresses. Others have been seen to jump over twenty feet from mallard nests in eucalyptus tree crotches, hitting benches or hard ground below, getting up and waddling down to the Lake with the hens. I have never observed nor seen proof of any duck carrying its young by bill from a nesting site.

Wildlife in a TV studio

Showing off wild animal pets for the TV studio cameras may become routine performance for zoo and museum staffers. As urban park naturalists we were invited to many kinds of shows.

106

Our animal "guests" have ranged from snakes to ducks and ducklings, young hawks and owls, raccoons, skunks, and opossums —and I may have overlooked a few others.

Among the problems and even hazards of introducing wild animals to TV studios are flood lights, other unprepared studio performers, and noisy protests or violent struggles when the animal guests find themselves exposed to such a strange, frightening situation.

Snakes, lizards, turtles, and tortoise are ideal subjects before studio cameras and bright lights, providing they have an experienced handler. They rarely produce loud noises and are generally easy to control. But even they can throw a studio into panic as when a big constrictor attacked San Diego Zoo curator Charlie Shaw on a local science broadcast, severely slashing his forearm.

We were once called upon to appear in the filming of a "Science in Action" show on television. The show was entitled "Animals on the Move." David Farrow, Jr., then assistant naturalist, and I were asked to bring some Lake Merritt pintails and demonstrate the banding of ducks and how it is used in tracing migrations. We were told, somewhat to our surprise, to be prepared for an all-day session.

The first setback of the show occurred at 9 a.m. with the death of a fresh-water eel which was to illustrate eel migration with the help of a large wall map. The eel was allowed to remain in the tank propped on a small rock. A big steelhead, which barely fitted in another small tank, was carefully watched all day for signs of passing out and was rejuvenated by some ice cubes at noon.

I was puzzled by a large spherical plastic bowl of dry moss sitting on a table and concluded it was a prop left over from a previous show. I was surprised later in the day to see the director with his head in the bowl directing his camera- and light-men through a mouthpiece connected with their headsets. The moss evidently cushioned the sound from reverberating through the studio.

The various preparations consumed so much time that the first "dry run" rehearsal didn't come off until about 10:30 and the actual filming didn't start until 11:30 so that the last ten minutes of the half-hour show were put off until after lunch.

In the process of being made up for the show, I asked if I could wear my uniform hat, but, after consultation, it was

announced that I couldn't wear it. However, after they turned lights and camera on my bald head, someone told me to get it and try it for looks. There were no further objections so I kept it on for the entire filming.

Lack of a simple fact or figure can cause a serious hangup in the show. This script called for me to estimate the distance flown by a duck returning to Lake Merritt from "some far northern point." I chose Nome, Alaska, and then found no one knew the mileage between these points. I guessed about 3,000 miles for the ducks' half-circle route which curves inland and does not follow the coast, but we had to know for sure. A quiet unidentified woman who sat in the corner volunteered to get this information. About three hours later she returned. After calling the public library and an airline serving Alaska, she finally got the mileage from someone at the Academy of Sciences who actually measured it off on a map—2400 miles from Nome to Oakland.

Later that afternoon during closeup shots, Dr. Earl S. Herald, narrator of "Science in Action," was simultaneously chewed by a pallid bat and a pintail, both on camera. The prevalence of rabies in a dormant form among bats wasn't so well known then. Happily this bat wasn't a carrier. Herald just let the animal chew away until the cameraman and the director thought they had enough film.

Finally the show got taped to everyone's satisfaction, to be shown later that evening. Dave and I and two very tired ducks were released. We both agreed that we preferred our normal park naturalist duties to those involved in TV educational broadcasts.

Bees, Beekeepers, and a Mothbreeder

*T*he hole-in-the-wall beehive paid off from the very beginning. The idea of a beehive in the wall was not new. Bible history describes how peasants housed their bees in the outer walls of their dwelling to protect them from marauding animals or humans. We had already observed how some nature centers had cleverly incorporated this beehive-in-the-wall idea as fascinating public exhibits. The bees simply required some sort of tunnel entrance to the out-of-doors, and it shouldn't open on a patio or walk or at too low a level.

Where in the world of "nature next door" can you, teacher or parent, find better live lessons in sociology, economics, and ecology than the beehive? First, you have your basic concept of pollination of flowers demonstrated by these conspicuous little workers. "So what? I heard all that stuff!" exclaims the sophisticated individualist in the group.

109

"O.K.," fires back the well-informed teacher, "how long could you live without hamburgers or apple pie?"

This gut-level approach brings looks of real concern to youthful faces, even the young upstarts. Now, a few simple facts once known to every rural child must be explained. Without the services of bees there wouldn't be clover and alfalfa to create beefsteaks and hamburger, or apples or cherries, or melons for hot summer days. In fact, starvation would soon face most of the world's population, including well-fed American kids like the youngsters who had heard it all before.

If you wish to distinguish and point out the drones, or boy bees, you better not wait until fall or winter to visit the hive; they just aren't there. Drones are produced only to mate with the virgin queen and actually only very few ever have that opportunity. From her one mating flight the queen stores enough sperm to fertilize tens of thousands of eggs over a lifetime of two to four years. Yet, only recently have we heard about frozen sperm banks for human reproduction. Otherwise the drones stand idly about, demanding food but contributing nothing to the work of the hive. No wonder they are allowed to starve after a while. What a lesson for youth of today! But, be careful; don't suggest Dad starve if he can't find a job!

Everyone knows about the bees' honey savings accounts to be used during lean seasons. As bees were among the earliest animal servants of man, carefully housed and jealously guarded even within human dwellings, how their thrifty habits must have been admired and even imitated by their human masters! How much we teach from their example today depends on our powers of persuasion and the backgrounds and attitudes of the audience. It may be too late to preach against public welfare, but you can compare the bees' habits to social security and savings accounts! And I think it might be the time to revive the old pioneer custom of "food banks" in the minds of listeners, in fact, for all American voters and all government officials you can reach.

Man against bee

So, if honey bees are absolutely essential to our survival, who is their greatest enemy today, the menace that could destroy the food chain and bring us starvation? That enemy is man himself!

Yes, despite the bee's formidable array of natural enemies—mites, ants, wax moths and certain birds and mammals—man looms as the greatest. Pesticides sprayed across pastures, croplands, and orchards to control injurious insects all too often reach this little insect servant, the honey bee. The essential coordination between the pest controller, farmer, and beekeeper does not always exist. The Department of Agriculture now pays large sums to reimburse beekeepers for part of such losses caused by pesticides. But that may not replace in time the hives so essential to fertilize crops. Because of such losses and other adverse factors, there have recently been such severe shortages of bees for crop fertilization that beekeepers have rushed their hives at premium rates from state to state. So, as we admire the bee of the exhibition hive, the occupation of beekeeping must be encouraged so that we may continue to reap the benefits of this incredible insect friend.

Fortunately, at the Natural Science Center, William B. Crump, a carpenter who also kept bees, volunteered to construct and install an exhibition hive. Installing such a bee colony is a simple trick, at least as performed by a professional. First, Mr. Crump went inside the Center and taped black paper across the viewing window to delude the bees into thinking they were moving into a nice dark chamber. Then he hung the box containing the swarm close to the outside entrance holes. A few scout bees explored the cavity, emerging shortly to signal "all clear—ready for occupancy." The queen, followed by her attendants and a few hundred workers, immediately entered. When the new tenants constructed a certain amount of honeycomb, the curtains were pulled aside, and the bees stayed on even if somewhat dismayed by the light on their private lives.

The first swarm of honey bees turned out to be an enigma— even to experts in the Alameda County Beekeepers' Association. On Mother's Day, a large swarm left this hive-in-the-wall after two days of hectic preswarming activity around the hive. They attached themselves to the nearest branch of a pine tree some fifty feet from the colony and within three feet of a heavily traveled crosswalk.

This was a magnetic attraction. Many youngsters and some grownups insisted on lingering close to the suspended swarm, and thanks to the bees' preoccupation with swarming problems, no one was stung. We asked a beekeeper who was building up his stock to come after the swarm. Again these bees proved baffling because they moved that evening, and again the next, from their park site to nearby gardens before the beekeeper overtook them.

111

As swarms revolve around the new queen, who departs the mother colony with a large following of workers, it is essential to keep your eye on that personality. A branding with red nail polish always helped the public to find the queen at the Center hive. She may remain through fall and winter, but with burgeoning spring crops and zooming hive populations, there must be a division of the colony—or swarming. This the beekeepers can predict by watching for the large queen cells in which future queens are being carefully nutured on royal jelly. Actually, only one virgin queen will survive after hatching. There's room for only one top cat in the house!

This fecund colony launched three more swarms—the last on Memorial Day when people were also "swarming" in the favorite location of the swarm on the same pine branch on the crosswalk only four feet from the ground. These swarms were noticeably smaller than the first so the incredible supply of new blood was finally running low. After each swarm, the mass of bees remaining in the wall hive was reduced, but always there remained a mass sufficient to cover the estimated two feet of comb already built down from the top of the panel.

The hive-in-the-wall continued as the second-best live animal show in the Center, outranked only by the snakes-in-the-wall. But this large box-like compartment, six feet high, two feet wide, and eight inches deep gradually proved difficult to maintain. When the bee-moth or wax-moth occasionally penetrated the outer defenses and infested the hive, it was an extremely laborious task to remove the inner box lining to clean and sterilize it so a smaller "demonstration frame" was mounted to replace it.

The honey give-away

After a successful "bee year," some forty to fifty pounds of honey had to be removed from the hole-in-the-wall to make room for a new year of activity. The Natural Science Center honey crop couldn't be sold. It was too much of a mixture of nectars, gathered all around Lakeside Park and in nearby gardens. Besides, it was produced in housing that couldn't be inspected by customary methods so we had to give it away. The first year, Mr. Crump and some other beekeepers suggested that the honey should be dispensed freely among visitors during a "free sample open house."

The "honey give-away" was scheduled for the first weekend following the fall rehabilitation of the hive. Boxes of crackers,

112

spoons, knives, and paper napkins were provided on a folding table, together with three quart jars of honey. Mr. Crump and associates beamed with pride and pleasure as the first visitors responded to their invitation to sample the product of "the Science Center Bees."

But there were pitfalls in the honey orgy—real sticky ones. Honey sampling on crackers is an art. If it proved difficult for the adults, it was just too much to expect of the younger set. Oh, they went for it, but with reckless enthusiasm which speedily led to disaster.

Little gobs of honey stuck to the floor, chairs, display cases— just about everywhere around the Center auditorium. Unsuspecting visitors uttered expressions of disgust when their feet refused to come up for the next step. And some who sat on the chairs near the "honey table" found the chairs threatened to follow them out of the building.

"Never again. It just won't work. People are too messy. Gad, what a mess. What'll the custodian say? Guess we'd better clean some up." With such comments, the much-heralded honey give-away idea came to an inglorious end.

Visitors who either wanted to know about keeping bees or how to get rid of bees compelled us to learn more about these insects. This led to the Alameda County Beekeepers using the Center one evening each month for their regular meeting. It even led to the discovery of an important public official known as "The County Bee Inspector"—an officer many city dwellers have never heard about.

I made a casual study of "The Typical Beekeeper." This type was usually male, between middle age and elderly, and of European ancestry. If he were married, his spouse was usually involved in his beekeeping. If she didn't actually handle the hives, she had to help in the preserving, marking, and marketing of honey. She also had to help explain, and sometimes pacify, the neighbors if the insects got out of line.

Beekeeping is not limited to commercial producers. There is the father-son team with just one or two hives for the family supply or to help the boy on a science project. There were some Future Farmers of America and 4-H Club boys and girls who often came to the meetings. Such a meeting was really a revelation for city-oriented folks as it brought together widely different types of "livestock farmers." With more city and suburban ordinances excluding poultry and livestock, here was a domestic animal that city dwellers could still keep. In fact successful bee colonies were reported in downtown Oakland within a few blocks from Lake Merritt and Lakeside Park.

We also learned of some neighborhood problems that urban beekeepers faced. The toilet habits of honey bees often caused more conflict with one's neighbors than did their tempers or stings. It was all due to the instinctive house-broken habit of this dainty insect. The bee empties its little bowels once it has flown a certain distance from the hive. And this distance often happens to be right over the neighbor's wash lines. All of which means that the successful beekeeper must place his hives in such a position that the bees' bathroom falls over a relatively unused area.

When bees swarm

Actually, physical attacks on the neighbors are usually few and rare. But when spring swarming season arrives, a different sort of bee movement may cause consternation in the neighborhood, even though the bees may not sting anyone. Each and every swarm must find a new home, according to nature's plan for the honey bee. And this home must be some sort of secure cavity. Man's own dwellings offer many kinds of cavities such as eaves, chimneys,

garages, etc. The scouts that accompany each swarm are uncannily adept at finding such places while the queen and a few thousand workers await the good word from their housing scouts. These scouts never ring bells or knock on doors to inquire if they will be welcome tenants.

Frantic calls besiege the beekeeper. "Can you come and get your swarm right away? Yes, they must be yours. You are the only one around here who keeps bees. They're coming in our windows, and my husband says he'll phone the police if you don't take them away."

In spring and summer other desperate appeals for relief from honey bee swarms threaten the tranquility of every known bee-keeper. Police departments, fire companies, pounds, animal shelters, mayors, city managers, and councilmen all receive such calls from citizens who believe their local authorities should "get those bees out of the yard." Anyone who operates a nature center with a bee display must know who takes care of bee swarms. We were fortunate in having as assistant naturalist a professional beekeeper, Lionel Kett, who performed nobly in counseling and comforting these callers—even putting them in touch with beekeepers who may dislodge their invaders.

All beekeepers do not want these escaped swarms. Some kindly retired fellows will answer such calls to give aid and comfort. Other beekeepers who are accomplished high climbers, carpenters, wreckers, and fumigators will accept such invitations for regular fees. But the park naturalist staff is limited in the help we can give because we can only go after bees which are on city property.

One morning bees greeted us in the Natural Science Center lobby. We further observed that there were more bees in every part of the building. Mr. Kett made straight for the hole-in-the-wall hive and found that the big picture window on the inside wall had been smashed by an overnight intruder. We wondered how the bees had reacted to this nocturnal attack on their privacy. Then we realized that a human predator of this nature might well have committed other depredations.

Sure enough. Directly across the auditorium, the even larger picture window of the rattlesnakes had been smashed. Several pieces littered the floor while other segments of glass remained in place. But the partial inner glass panel or "second barrier" had been spared. Although this panel was only eighteen inches high, the lethargic rattlers had respected it and remained in the set. We quickly removed the snakes to the safety of a portable box, and then turned back to the problem of rounding up a few hundred disturbed bees. Many of the bees had already returned to the vicinity of their cracked window so it was a simple matter to place a sheet of mat-board over the entire inside face of the hive.

This particular human predator, with such a warped instinct of destruction, was never identified, but over the years we have watched the Center bees wreak vengeance on humans who attacked from the outside. Occasionally some passing youngsters would spot the bees clustered about their small outer doorways located at six and ten feet above the ground. What a chance to get a cheap thrill and to show the gang they weren't chicken.

A few small stones or dirt clods might fail to get an immediate reaction from the bees so the kids would move in a little closer. Sometimes we would hear the bombardment and chase off the ill-advised vandals. But on certain occasions, the bees had reacted first, and we heard yells of pain and fright before we could intercept the youngsters. Or we might reach the doors just in time to see several sprinting across the street, still yelling and swatting at their pursuers! We know *they* will not come back for more.

Lessons in sociology, economics, and ecology are graphically presented each year to thousands of visiting school children who come to the Natural Science Center. The elementary bee-and-flower concept is illustrated for the younger pupils. Examples of the rewards of good teamwork and thrift are conspicuous in the abundant honey store and performance of various hive duties. Did nature experiment with communism in the bee society? What happens to the shiftless drones once they complete their small contribution to the reproductive life of the queen is a rude shock to many a child, teacher, and parent.

Live insect displays

Except for bees, and an occasional successful ant farm, it has been my observation that live insect displays have been grossly neglected by the typical nature center. Pinned and neatly labelled insect specimens, particularly butterflies and moths, are common enough. But how often have you seen a live insectarium? Even large museums and zoos seldom offer such an exhibit. We often

116

attempted, and sometimes succeeded, in showing a moth or butterfly metamorphosis from caterpillar to cocoon to adult, but junior aides have seldom wanted to assume the day-to-day care of an insect. So when Frank dropped in one day and promised to collect and display live insects as well as rehabilitate our pinned insect collection, we readily gave him a chance.

Frank showed up each morning and managed to keep a large work table in the reference library covered with insects, killing jars, pinning boards, and portable cases. He also left this work frequently to answer the telephone, answer questions at the office door, even to give impromptu "snake talks" for youth groups whenever the other junior aides were not ready and willing. The interruptions on some days exceeded the time left for his special assignment. The clutter and mess in the library remained except for enforced weekend partial cleanups. We of the staff just couldn't seem to keep Frank on a single track—that of reorganizing the collection.

But it was the lure of field collecting that really kept the budding entomologist from getting much done indoors. Someone would mention seeing a moth, a butterfly, perhaps a caterpillar, or chrysalis, and away he would go with his net and a jar. He might be gone an hour or two, but the catch he brought in was likely to be interesting—maybe even a rare trophy. Then, if possible, we would try to get Frank to install it in a live insectarium for all visitors to admire. This meant another daily search for the insect's special food.

Daylight butterfly chasing wasn't enough for this eager bug hunter. One morning he showed up late and red-eyed. We asked, "How come?"

"I stayed up until 2 a.m. breeding!" He had tethered out female silk moths, the *polyphemus,* and hung around to see if the male's reputedly master scent-tracking organs were as keen as reported. They were, he assured us with an air of great triumph. After hours of patient waiting, the male moth had appeared and mated with a tethered female.

But Frank's greatest accomplishment of the few weeks he spent at the Center was not in mating moths, or hatching eggs, and certainly not in rearranging collections. It came quite unsolicited and unexpected. It was Frank's miscellaneous array of specimens and equipment spread over the library which really led to this other achievement.

117

Students from a local state college who were seeking bird, insect, and native plant identification came to the Center. Among these students was a bewildered and floundering middle-aged man we will call Jones. He discovered Frank, and it was a case of infatuation on sight—that is, infatuation of Jones with this bug-hunting talent of Frank's. The older nature student decided that this boy could help him understand the world of insects, and also help him set up a collecting and study project that would certainly earn him points with the "prof."

This platonic affair of the bug collectors grew and flourished from week to week. The relief and gratitude of Jones was something to watch as Frank helped him to develop his project and term report. This help paid off for Frank. His student was evidently pretty well off and anxious to pay for services rendered. One day he presented Frank with a magnificent new butterfly volume; another time with an expensive textbook on entomology. And Frank seemed to have plenty of cash for equipment and collecting trips.

Frank's researches finally took him to the University of California's Department of Entomology. Here he became absorbed in the academic atmosphere. He was received as a new volunteer laboratory aide and a useful contributor of fresh specimens from the field. So our erstwhile staff entomologist, Frank, stopped coming to the Center. We sadly gathered up the jumble of unclassified insects, assigned another volunteer to collect tomato leaves daily for the sphinx moth larvae in the screen cage, and wondered when another dedicated bug collector would cross our doorstep.

Children learn bee-lore from Asst. Naturalist Lionel Kett at science center hive-in-wall.

Snakes Alive—and Other Scaly Ones

Would *you* want to bring a snake into your home but don't quite trust them? A harmless one, of course. Does your child threaten to leave home if he can't keep a snake as a pet? Are you fond of picnics and walks in the country but terrified of stepping on a snake, perhaps a poisonous kind?

Most North American snakes are harmless. All snakes are very clean animals, if given proper quarters. Their scales do not harbor fleas or lice, like so many other household pets. Mites can attack them under their scales, but may be controlled with oil baths or miticides. Snakes don't have voices to awaken the neighbors early in the morning. They do not even have to be fed or watered daily. A good meal each week is sufficient for most species. They can be conveniently transported with the family when it moves—or be taken unobtrusively to office, classroom, or party when desirable. A word of warning about this latter habit, however. Never, never produce your snakes suddenly where not expected or welcome. This mistake can cost you a black eye, a lawsuit, or social ostracism—and may even cause severe injury to some panicky bystander.

The problem is that there just are not enough snakes to go around in our spreading metropolitan areas. Some species have already been wiped out in and around large cities, even though plentiful habitat and food remains for them. If every boy or girl wanting a pet snake were to follow through and somehow acquire one, that would seal their doom. Snakes seldom breed well in captivity, which means the hapless specimens you find in pet shops are mostly live-caught. They are often half starved when you pay the price and take them home, and your purchase has sent more youngsters out to ransack the wood and field for the few remaining snakes.

If you must keep a native snake, however you come by it, I suggest that you turn it loose before the end of the summer to enable it to fatten itself on natural food before winter hibernation. And if it will not accept food, either live or inanimate, while a pet, I urge you to release it much sooner. When fall comes most captive snakes, lizards, and turtles do not find suitable hibernation conditions. Their keepers naturally want them to continue eating, and this usually leads to fatal metabolic disturbances.

A harmless snake or other small, native reptile in a classroom terrarium is an exhibit of interest and value to many children. It may even teach the teacher something, once forced to accept it. So, my snake-loving friend, why not share your captured or purchased snake with the entire class, and then make a big event— perhaps a class field trip—out of the occasion when you turn it loose?

Some true snake stories

The incidents and anecdotes that follow are mostly unrelated to one another, but they may help to dispel some of your notions about the serpent kind. They may even convince you that snakes are better left where seen in woodland, chaparral, meadow, pond, or stream for a number of reasons.

Toward the end of a Thanksgiving afternoon naturalist program, an excited lady came out of the Science Center to announce that a big struggle was taking place in the "Snakes Alive" display. I was somewhat surprised to find that the king snake had selected one of the largest garter snakes for his holiday menu.

Quite a few persons had gathered before the front of the case, and I had difficulty in getting into the case to intercede. The California king snake had the garter snake by the head in such a fast grip that I found it impossible to break the hold with a pencil tip. He was also tightly enmeshed in several coils of the king snake.

After incurring one tooth puncture from the king snake's jaws, I decided to give up any attempt to separate them. Anyway garter snakes are easier to find than king snakes.

Fascinated visitors again gathered around and remained until the building was closed. At that time, the king snake had barely ingested the head of the garter snake.

By the next morning there was no trace of the garter snake outside the king snake. Three days later when mice were given to all snakes in the case, this same king snake immediately seized and ate two mice although obviously still distended from his garter snake meal.

One spring a scoutmaster donated a California king snake about thirty inches long. He said it had been in captivity for some weeks and had refused all food, but it appeared in fair condition.

This king continued to refuse the weekly offerings of mice put into the common cage it shared with gopher and garter snakes. It appeared to be staging a hunger strike, as some snakes do. Then one day in mid-July when I was taking out snakes for a day camp tour, I discovered this king in the initial stage of consuming a medium-sized gopher snake at least as long as itself. The gopher snake was still struggling violently. The king's efforts to consume the gopher snake continued until noon when it had all but some six or eight inches down, and then suddenly it regurgitated the whole meal!

The anticlimax came the next day when we opened the box to display the snakes and two large alligator lizards just brought in the previous day. These lizards were missing, in addition to a smaller blue-bellied lizard. The king snake had another bulge in his mid-section.

A few days later the kids at Grass Valley Day Camp had captured a splendid king snake three feet long. The director offered it to me in exchange for a young king about twelve inches long. After some hesitation, I fell for the larger specimen and placed the big king in a small box with the gopher snake, garter snake, and a newly-acquired blue-bellied racer.

Forty-five minutes later, upon opening the snake box in front of some hundred children at the next day camp, I was shocked to find no racer, but a distinct bulge occupying a good part of the king's body. There was even a portion of tail protruding from king's mouth.

Snake surprises

The ventilation screen had been removed from a small snake display box on a table at the Rotary Natural Science Center and a medium-sized king snake was missing. Clues to this minor crime were soon forthcoming. A gardener reported seeing a small boy with a king snake in the Park. Upon inquiry, the boy stated he had found it in the Park.

The Snow Museum called. Had we missed a king snake? Two small boys had just left there after persuading members of the staff to pay them eighty cents for a king snake. The description fitted the two urchins seen flitting in and out to the Science Center earlier in the day and the boy seen with the snake—both youngsters riding a single bicycle. Our friends at the Snow Museum promised to hold the bartered snake for us.

Early the next morning, one of these young lads appeared very contritely at the Center and tried to explain that his friend had really stolen the snake and that he just found out about it. Since we lacked actual witnesses to the theft, we could only lecture the boy and turn him out with a warning.

The manager of one of East Oakland's industrial plants called. Small snakes from an adjacent field were invading his factory and panicking some workers. He thought they were harmless species, but many of his employees were convinced they were rattlesnakes. The telephone description was inconclusive, but he already had one pickled in a jar of alcohol to bring to the Center for identification.

The manager and his foreman brought the snake to the Science Center. The reptile was a young gopher snake, and we explained to their satisfaction how we recognized it. The gentlemen left much happier knowing it was a harmless snake, but still wondered what formula would effectively close their doors to all such reptiles, good or bad.

As for us, we felt pleased that we had been able to forestall serious labor troubles in this plant of two hundred and fifty employees.

There had been one of those snake calls that stirred more than ordinary interest. This youngster said he had a medium-sized California king snake and was thinking of donating it to us. The only hitch was that the snake had a "bad cut on the tail."

We advised the boy to bring in the reptile rather than try to much home doctoring. Since we rarely have too many king snakes, we were quite anxious to get this one in time to save it. In the midst of the lunch period, the boy arrived with his king snake in a crude home-made box, the top weighted down by heavy blocks of wood. Boy, snake, and box had traveled some distance by bus.

We quickly ushered the boy into the Library where the customary vacation staff of young helpers were gathered. Off came the lid as we hastened to see what sort of injury this king snake had. The room was tense as we awaited the diagnosis.

To our surprise we found the snake's anal opening smothered tightly in layers of bandaids. The reptile's discomfort was quite evident as natural elimination had been stopped. The chagrin of this lad was even more obvious, and we really felt sorry that his ignorance of snake anatomy was revealed in the presence of other boys. Anyhow, the bandages were removed as quickly and painlessly as possible, and the relieved snake was permitted to join the other large snakes in the wall-inset serpentarium.

This boy's ignorance of snake anatomy seemed far less shocking to us. Many grownups have asked us if the Gila monster really has an anus. Of course it has! These gullible people have swallowed an old Western folk tale to the contrary. Spiking such nature fables is an almost daily duty of a naturalist.

Snake escapees

Jackie, a friend from a local museum, borrowed a medium-sized gopher snake to take on her tour to Children's Hospital. After summer "conditioning" by handling, we thought all our snakes were quite tame and resigned to fondling and display.

It proved otherwise with this gopher snake, which we will call "Troubles." In the midst of excited young admirers at the hospital, he became confused and fearful and bit both Jackie and a child. This was somewhat embarrassing because some of the hospital staff were dubious about wild animal pets being there.

Troubles was determined to pursue his criminal career. At Jackie's home that evening, he got out of his carrying case and moved under the door to the opposite side of the duplex. There a frantic search got under way about midnight, with aspirins and sedatives passed around to the neighbor ladies. Finally, Troubles was found and returned to his box which was rendered escape-proof. The next morning this errant snake, unaware of the panic, explanations, and apologies left in his wake, was safely back with his friends in the Science Center display.

A local high school science teacher had a most harrowing adventure right in his classroom. It all got started when a large gopher snake being kept for class observation escaped from its display box. During the after-school search, it was seen just as it disappeared through a crack in the classroom wall.

The teacher and one of his student assistants went to work on the crack. A wire hook was tried in hopes of extracting the snake, but the cagey reptile merely crawled farther back behind the nearest joist. In desperation, the snake seekers got wrecking tools from the custodian and started on the wall. They had to remove a section of molding and pull out an entire panel before they found the snake. This was hard to explain to the principal the next morning.

The problem of coaxing snakes out from under car seats and dashboards is by no means a new one. I recall a local news item of a prowl car officer who picked up a gopher snake at the home of a frantic citizen, only to have the snake escape under the car seat and defy all efforts of officers and garage hands to extract it. Not until the next day did the snake crawl from its retreat. The police department refused to say if they had posted a round-the-clock watch in the automobile.

Such an experience involving a snake-shy wife was recounted by a prominent zoologist who conducted a television program. The zoologist had somewhat hastily packed in the family car a large tropical snake which was scheduled to appear on his television program later that day. It was first necessary to pick up his wife at the airport. But, en route, he found that the reptile had somehow escaped from its carton and was comfortably ensconced behind the wires and instruments of the dashboard.

The scientist was confronted with a difficult decision. He knew his wife abhorred snakes, but she also resented being left waiting at the airport. The situation clearly demanded a gamble on the snake remaining hidden on its perch while he took care of his wife. And this it did, although he admitted he sweated all the way home, with his wife's legs a few inches from the giant reptile. Oh yes, it crawled out soon afterward for the television program.

Another local science teacher had an extraordinary experience. He had confined together in his classroom terrarium both a medium-sized frog and a young garter snake about eight inches long. Under the usual procedures in such circumstances, the garter snake might be expected to size up the amphibian as potential food.

But this particular frog was a freethinker. One morning the teacher and students were astonished to find the snake part way down the frog's gullet. It proved quite a mouthful too, even for this enterprising frog, and required most of that day for the forward half of the snake to be assimilated in order that the terminal half could be swallowed. All this did disrupt other class activities to some extent, but it was an eloquent, if somewhat distasteful, example of how nature can sometimes reverse its rules.

Snakes people brought us

Early one morning an agitated and hurried man drove up, got out of his car, and handed us a small jar containing a young gopher snake less than a foot long. He was anxious to determine the species and to know whether or not it was harmless. He introduced himself as a physician and said he had driven from Hayward to settle this matter.

This little gopher snake had bitten both a small boy and his sister after they had found it and handled it awhile. Frantic parents captured the ten-inch reptile, phoned the family doctor, and started for the county hospital with their frightened children.

At the hospital, they got immediate attention in the emergency ward and wound up with shots of "serum" for the bites.

125

Just what kind of serum the doctor wasn't sure, but we have a hunch it was rattlesnake serum. It was unfortunate that no one paid much attention to the matter of identifying the offending snake until the next day when the family doctor notified them that the snake had been identified as harmless.

Miss Diane, a lovely titian-haired professional dancer, walked in and asked if we could board her six-foot boa constrictor until she could trade it for another. She had counted on incorporating this snake into a new act, and had been assured by the dealer, who charged $35, that it was "the gentle kind." But the boa didn't get the word and tried to bite her during the very first rehearsal. Being a better dancer than snake charmer, she immediately decided to turn it in on a tamer, more tractable specimen. We didn't really feature exotic snakes, but Diane had a charming way about her so we obligingly agreed to board and display the boa until "trade-in" time.

Each spring a great influx of snakes is brought in by friends and amateur collectors. These include gopher, garter, and king snakes, rattlesnakes, and less often the tiny ring-necked and sharp-tailed, or the restless, irritable racers.

This particular spring rattlesnake donations seemed to over-balance all the others. As we had three or four live through the winter, we didn't particularly want any more. But in spite of us, they came, including several babies. Three were picked up on successive weekend visits by a local family to their Russian River country cabin. Though we tried to show no enthusiasm over the first donation, they still returned with more of the "baby buzzies." They just didn't have the heart to kill them but couldn't leave them around.

The young rattlers were put into the wall display case along with the large ones since we couldn't think of any other safe place for them. But we had forgotten about the wide cracks in the pine boards behind the matboard "scenery" panels. One morning when I opened the Center front door, there was one of the baby rattlers trying to coil and threaten any intruders. Another was found in a far corner of the auditorium. All we recovered and moved to a safer display spot and steps were taken to fill the cracks. However, our janitor did get quite upset when he heard about it.

Snake births

Over the years of reptile exhibits in the Science Center snake

126

section, there have been some unexpected "blessed events," most notable of which was the birth of about sixty garter snakes. A third of them were stillborn, but we had quite a time disposing of forty little snakes after featuring them on display for a few weeks. Snake babies are difficult to feed although they are known to take some insects.

Rattlesnakes, like the harmless garter snakes, are supposed to be viviparous—that is, to give birth to live young. I was startled, therefore, when passing the rattlesnake hole-in-the-wall one morning, to find that a medium-sized Western Rattlesnake was laying eggs. Apparently this individual hadn't gotten the word on reproduction for her species because it was certainly an atypical situation. Three eggs had already been deposited on the gravel floor of the cage, and it was evident from the writhing contortions of the female that more would be coming.

The eggs were leathery with some thick mucous covering, and there was some slight movement in two of them. Something in there wanted out. Should we take a hand? Baby rattlers are notoriously difficult to feed. But on the other hand, we were curious. After watching further efforts of the mother to produce more of these ill-conceived eggs, we decided to try.

First we used the specially-cut piece of plyboard and the snakestick—the tools with which we move about the rattlers and then restrict them to one half of their case while clean-ups are performed in the other half. Then, having safely removed from reach all the snakes except the would-be mother, we proceeded to "operate" on two of her eggs with the end of the hook on the snake-handling stick. Very gingerly we broke through a slight aperture on one egg and were rewarded by the gradual emergence of a tiny rattlesnake. We tackled the second egg, with similar results, and wondered how many successful "Caesareans" had been performed on rattlesnake eggs.

By this time the female was on the verge of producing another egg so we withdrew from the scene. She laid two more eggs, but they appeared tougher and smaller than those we had hatched so we "let sleeping snakes lie."

The baby rattlers soon dried off and began to crawl around and take their place in this tight little community. They would curl on, under, or alongside any of the other large snakes. Their own mother showed no particular interest in them, which is the usual rule among snakes. They did present an additional hazard in the maintenance of the "snake pit" in the wall panel because they coiled and blended so perfectly with the gravel floor of the case. It is all too easy to overlook such youngsters while carefully avoiding the bigger snakes in cleaning or feeding operations. And their bites could be very unpleasant, if not so dangerous as the bite of a full-grown specimen.

We tried to rear our own mice and rats to feed the snakes. Even though a local laboratory engaged in cancer research very kindly supplied us with experimental mice, we were reluctant to use them except as breeders. The lab officials assured us their mice carried no toxic injections. Still, when we first started using these mice, we lost several harmless snakes and several rattlesnakes, the very same snakes which had partaken of the lab mice.

On another occasion we were short of grown mice to feed the snakes and resorted to some fresh lab mice. Two days later, the biggest gopher snake and a king snake died in convulsions. So we gave the breeding stock of white mice warmer quarters and more privacy in pairs in order that only the offspring without laboratory experience would be used for snake food.

Hatching gopher snakes

"Paul, Paul, the snakes are hatching."

This startling news was brought into the Science Center in the early afternoon of September 10, 1966. One of the most devoted Junior Naturalist Aides discovered the great event in the Back Room.

It seemed long, long ago that a female gopher snake was noticed laying eggs, one at a time over a period of an entire afternoon. The date was July 22. Several of the "juniors" were present at the time, including two dedicated boy herpetologists. Immediately there arose a great debate on how to care for these snake eggs to insure their hatching. Mother snakes take no interest in their eggs after laying them in the proper environment. Many such eggs had been laid over the years in the serpentarium, even given tender, special "lay-away" treatment, but none had ever hatched normally.

As Paul and Dave, the snake specialists, argued louder and louder over the proper disposition of these precious nuggets, some arbitration was imperative. The boys had consulted books which contained rather meager reference to this seldom-practiced business of snake-egg care, so I phoned Dr. Robert Stebbins, one of the foremost herpetologists of North America.

Dr. Stebbins recommended placing the eggs in individual foil wrapping and hanging them in a moderately warm room. He did admit that of all his snake-egg treatments over the years, only a few had ever hatched. But Paul knew and admired this herpetologist and insisted that we follow his advice. Dave had heard of an entirely different method of putting the eggs in dampened paper toweling in individual air-tight lab jars. So the issue was still in conflict, but the solution was not difficult. We "bottled" four of the eight eggs and put them in view within a small snake cage. The remaining four we wrapped in foil and hung in the office closet near the heating plant. Now both Paul and Dave were reasonably satisfied.

On this memorable afternoon over six weeks later, someone had noticed a snake egg cracking or "pipping" in the bottle in the Back Room. So the entire lot were brought and spilled out gently on the office desk. All four were heaving gently and showing multiple cracks. A tiny head and tongue were beginning to protrude from one crack, surrounded by bubbly liquid.

On such rare occasions a naturalist always gets a picture. The one egg so near to hatching was taken outside, placed on a piece of colored cardboard, and photographed. Quite a circle of curious folks gathered around. In fact, it was necessary to ask them to move back a bit to allow full light to shine on the subject.

The next step was to broadcast the news—invite everybody to witness this event and share our pride and joy in this herpetological achievement. All four eggs had been replaced in their damp paper bedding on a tray on the library table. Number One had already revealed the entire head. But it was still hesitant to emerge into this big bright world. Perhaps it even became aware that it was the reason that scores of people were trooping into the room to see for themselves this blessed event. It seemed to prove once again that all the world loves an infant—even a baby snake.

At closing time that afternoon, only one young gopher snake was completely out of its egg. The remaining eggs in the bottles were replaced in the slightly-heated back room cage. It was the next afternoon before they had disgorged their little snakes, each between five and six inches long.

And the four eggs carefully wrapped in foil and hung in the closet? They eventually molded and had to be thrown out.

Reptiles you can love

"Don't you have some kind of reptile that doesn't slither or crawl, hiss or bite, shed its skin or have to be fed live bugs or worms?" a disturbed parent once asked me. Her young son had become obsessed with keeping a reptile pet. Many other visitors have similar inquiries. As park naturalists, we were expected to furnish satisfactory answers for both parent and child.

So we could say, "Yes, step into the mini-zoo and we'll introduce you to a couple of clean, friendly reptiles."

First we presented "Iggie," an eighteen-inch common or Mexican iguana which stared at visitors from his small, heated glass-fronted compartment. We had boarded other iguanas up to nearly five feet long but ordinarily refused most of these exotic reptiles or turned them over to the zoo.

Mexican iguanas are gentle, friendly, and clean. They do require heated quarters, a stump to climb, and a moderate amount of exercise. Most of them will thrive on lettuce and various soft fruits, with a mouse or a bit of raw beef to spice that diet from time to time.

The iguana must periodically shed his skin, usually in pieces and patches, but this doesn't detract too much from its appearance which is far from handsome by most human-rated animal styles. If frightened or badly handled the iguana may either bite or lash its rough-scaled tail so swiftly that considerable damage can result to any exposed skin within range. Many a captive iguana will go on a hunger strike, perhaps from the moment it arrives in its new home. It can be force-fed, even if its jaws clamp shut like a vise. I remember one monster that would accept only avocados. Did you ever price avocados out of season? Still, this big paisano is our favorite of all the lizard clan that still appear in pet stores.

There are other lizards like the tego, tokay gecko, and anoles. All are insect and meat eaters. If a mounting demand for them threatens their existence in their native countries, they could suddenly be placed on the endangered species list. California and Arizona, just to mention two progressive states in conservation, have already stopped collection of certain lizard species and placed limitations on others. Some lizards, snakes, and salamanders are even protected by federal law.

Our number one reptile pet, judged by popularity, gentleness, ease of feeding, cleanliness, and adaptability, was the desert tortoise. This could be any of the species of *Gopherus* which range from California to Florida. They are now all protected as endangered species, so they can no longer be purchased in pet stores. There are some exotic kinds of tortoises like the red-legged, star, and pancake species which are still sold by dealers.

The California desert tortoise *(Gopherus agassizi)* was the very first reptile to receive total protection under state law. Still, I would hesitate to guess the number of pets of this species kept in the San Francisco Bay Area alone — not to mention other cities and other states. Public zoos and museums may get permission to exhibit these fascinating reptiles. There hasn't been any concerted move by game agents to confiscate those in private hands, but some tortoise lovers have organized a "Tortoise Repatriation Service." These persons return to the desert various tortoises which have been donated, confiscated, or have escaped from their private keepers and have been picked up and brought to an approved collection center like a junior museum or zoo.

Most of these kidnapped desert dwellers do not live out their natural long lives in damp northern climates. They rarely mate under captive conditions, and, if they do, and go so far as to lay eggs, these rarely can be hatched.

There are two general schools of thought and procedure on keeping desert tortoises in northern climates. One school prefers the outdoor garden habitat; the second group of "amateur experts" keep their pets the year round in a house or basement habitat. The outdoor range is fine for the summer months when your "Gopherus" may choose its own vegetarian diet of lawn grasses, weeds, and what-have-you. But it had better have access to a snug box when temperatures drop and cold rains or snow set in. If all goes well, the tortoise's own metabolic controls will guide it into hibernation.

This first system hasn't always worked at Children's Fairyland in Oakland where over the years a succession of tortoises have been presented for display. Even despite open access to covered quarters filled with sand and leaves, many of these animals have died, apparently of pneumonia or similar symptoms, during the winter months.

At the Natural Science Center, quite different tortoise quarters have been provided by a glass-fronted, screen-topped box filled with sand and heated by a forty-watt hooded light bulb. Here three or four desert tortoises of various sizes and ages live under fairly uniform heat right through the year — with the light bulb turned off during hot spells.

131

Tortoise exercise and grazing was held each weekend on the lawn area right outside the museum doors. This was a good occupation for one of the younger naturalist aides. A big Mexican or common iguana was sometimes added to this lawn party to pep it up a bit.

Once in awhile, the foot-long, four-pound female tortoise would drop an egg or two. The eggs are oval, white, hard-shelled, and almost two inches long. They are laid in a three- or four-inch deep excavation dug by the female with her hind feet. She then leaves them alone, and it is believed they require about three months to hatch. The babies do not need maternal care.

Over the years, I cannot boast of ever having had a tortoise egg hatch. In fact, I know of only one bay area tortoise keeper who has succeeded—Miss M.

One day Miss M. phoned for advice after her pet tortoise laid a clutch of eggs. I told her what little I knew, such as packing them in sand in a sunny situation. Many weeks later, Miss M. announced her tortoise blessed events. She had even planned her annual vacation in order to be home during the critical days when the hatching would occur. I told her she now outranked all the tortoise experts I knew, but she never returned to fill us in on the progress of her little brood.

Desert tortoises are heavy drinkers and will even soak in shallow water, though I suspect they could drown in a deep pool. This leads to a warning to tortoise handlers. They may empty their bladders with a powerful stream that can douse you and a circle of admirers. Be careful.

Bambis, Pilfering Raccoons, and Blundering Possums

The local fox squirrels, whose ancestors were transplants from the eastern United States some decades ago, were wide awake all winter and starting another season of domestic activities in Lakeside Park. Ever since their introduction to the Eastbay in the early 1900's, these big handsome Eastern fox squirrels have had the parks pretty much to themselves squirrel-wise. The original tree squirrels—the gray squirrels—had been eliminated by epidemic diseases, leaving a vacuum.

Each year the fox squirrels built and occupied two nests— a rather bulky, airy nest of twigs and leaves in a deciduous oak for their summer residence, and a compact, tightly lined nest in an evergreen for the winter season. They preferred the dense redwoods in the nursery area, but would sometimes put their winter den in the crotch of a live oak. Occasionally, a more ingenious female would move into an old ornamental street light with a glass pane cracked out or even enlarge a hole in the roof of some building and carry in the bedding.

Late in the month of February, the park tree-trimming crew was not prepared for the violent attack launched upon it when the men climbed to the top of a big live oak to remove dead limbs and thin the branches. A mother fox squirrel had carefully placed her winter nest in a high crotch. She bitterly resented this intrusion, but she didn't quite dare to meet in personal encounter these husky humans with shiny hard hats and wicked looking pruning poles. So she leaped from branch to branch over their heads and released a urine spray on them. The crew and their foreman, a nature buff himself, soon concluded Mother Squirrel deserved to carry out her nesting in peace and the oak trimming could wait.

Later that spring another squirrel mother gave up her favorite nest site in a large pine after staging a delaying-action offensive against the same tree crew. The men had actually withdrawn and left the top branches where she had her carefully constructed winter nest. But she no longer felt secure with her babies there. Early the next morning, one of the nurserymen saw her loping along the walk into the nursery, half carrying and half dragging a baby under her chin. She continued along the walk and across the flower beds to the base of a large redwood. Up she went, baby still firmly gripped, and disappeared in the dense sheltering branches.

A few minutes passed and down she came, alone, and headed back across the nursery and through the park to the big pines. Soon she reappeared with another of her litter, carrying it also up into the redwood. This she repeated four times until she had the entire litter securely established in a new home.

That darling squirrel in the park—how often have you or your children been tempted to pick it up and cuddle it? We hope you've resisted the impulse and saved yourself a bad bite. Most park squirrels, fox, red or gray, are still wild animals. Oh, they may come to your hand or even climb up your leg for a walnut. That is usually the break-off point in their overtures. Like most rodents, they just don't appreciate petting or handling unless they have been hand-reared orphans.

"Hey, one of your squirrels just bit my little boy! You better get the squirrel before he bites someone else. Does my son have to take a rabies shot?"

That is just the kind of call that promises to spoil a beautiful day for the park naturalist.

134

Rabies, fortunately, is of low incidence among squirrels and other native rodents. That information will quiet somewhat the squirrel victim or his parents. But the responsible park official must still find that particular squirrel, catch it, and confine it for at least two weeks for observation. If it dies in that period, the head must be examined by a health clinic or lab. Did you ever try to identify and catch one squirrel in a park full of squirrels?

Raccoon antics

One summer day a citizen phoned to ask about feeding some baby raccoons. What he really wanted was to turn over the litter to us. They had been taken from an attic in a suburban home after their crying had kept the household awake all night and on edge all day.

We took these three cute babies which we guessed to be about six weeks old. They soon caught on to bottle-feeding and immediately became the prime attraction at the Natural Science Center. For the Fourth of July crowd we even bottle-fed them on a platform in the Duck Feeding area.

Later that month there was another desperate telephone appeal from a lady when a raccoon situation became critical with her. This lady and her husband lived on a hilltop lot surrounded by other homes but not too far from some undeveloped canyon land. They had been protecting and sometimes feeding a lady raccoon which took up residence about a year before in a big oak in the very center of their garden. Although there was a family dog, they generally managed to restrict it at night when Mrs. Raccoon was prowling about. This couple freely admitted to being "addicted to wild animals."

The crisis came when Mrs. Raccoon had become bolder and hungrier and had raided a next-door fishpond. The gentleman of that house uttered violent threats of punishment for this furry marauder, threats which smote the animal-loving souls of the neighbors. Then the crisis worsened when Mrs. Raccoon suddenly brought forth from the hollow in the live oak a litter of four wobbly babies. This was the point when we were summoned to live-trap this problem family and transfer them to some more secure, distant environment.

As we already had our hands full with the trio of raccoon youngsters, we thought of Bob, a teenage animal trapper and erstwhile raccoon tamer whose pet had recently escaped. He took the bait eagerly. It was understood he could keep or dispose of all the young raccoons he might catch if he would also remove the mother to some distant place.

About 10 o'clock that evening, the lady called. Mother Raccoon was in the trap, but her litter had been ordered back to safety within the hollow oak. Bob, the trapper, had left rather early in the evening and could not be reached at home. The lady asked if I would come up if further efforts to reach Bob failed.

The "further efforts" failed to find Bob or any members of his family and by 10:30 p.m. I was en route to the scene of trouble. There sat Mother Raccoon crouching dejectedly and completely filling the rectangular live trap. She appeared too humiliated to even growl until we all but laid hands on the trap. Her youngsters were nowhere to be seen. In fact, a flashlight search of the hollow in the oak from both entrances failed to disclose a hair of them, but they were probably huddled up in the den out of sight.

The most practical solution would have been to remove the female promptly to some distant place and trust to picking up the youngsters when they became hungry enough to come out looking for her. But we just couldn't bear to separate her so abruptly and completely from the litter. I had two smaller traps which I baited with chicken heads and placed one on either side of Mother in her

larger trap. We withdrew for the night, confidently expecting to have at least a couple of youngsters trapped by daybreak. We even threw a gunny sack over Mother to ward off the night chill.

Furry escape artist

The next morning another distress call came from the lady. Mother Raccoon was back in the tree with her litter, and the big trap had been somewhat taken apart. Even the smaller traps had been carefully sprung to protect the innocent.

The bigger trap was returned to the park during the day, and I repaired the wire trigger that the clever female practically tied in knots. How she had managed to open the double-fold-down end door remains a mystery. Trapper Bob had returned to the scene by this time and begged a second chance to tackle this wily beast. He was prepared to remain all night, if necessary.

An entire day and a night passed without further messages from the scene of action. While I welcomed the opportunity to step back to the role of "interested observer," I found curiosity getting the better of me. How was this besieged Mother Raccoon holding out against this array of human brains and equipment? On the second evening, I telephoned for a report.

There had been the greatest "raccoon circus" yet witnessed in the garden that evening when Bob returned to carefully reset the three traps and then hide out to await the captures. Soon after dark Mother Raccoon emerged from the oak and began to inspect the live traps. Apparently the chicken head bait was too tantalizing to give up easily. On orders from mother, the four babies remained perched on the oak trunk looking on the scene. For further protection, the mother had dragged a small but heavy ceramic squirrel from a position on the oak trunk above the lower den opening, down the sloping trunk where she wedged it into the narrow den doorway in an obvious effort to keep her children from using that entrance so near the traps.

Mother Raccoon decided she had these nuisance contrivances figured out. Cautiously she crawled into the large trap, keeping her rear anatomy pushed up against the drop door and slightly protruding until she could reach over the trip pedal and seize the chicken head beyond. Then she gingerly withdrew from the trap, clutching her prize. All the while the youngsters danced up and down on the oak trunk and purred and squealed in eagerness to descend and share in the fun. But mother was adamant.

Next, the smaller live traps were studied and then attacked by the hungry female. But her girth was just too much to admit her any distance or to a point where she could extract the bait. She pushed them around awhile in disgust until they were sprung and overturned. At 2 a.m. the spectators in the house grew weary. Even Bob was ready to throw in the sponge. So the flood light was switched off and the raccoons left in glorious darkness and free to indulge in any mischief they might choose.

The animal-loving couple held an early breakfast conference. A major decision was reached. Mother Raccoon had shown such tenacity and intelligence in outwitting her human landlords in their eviction schemes that she had earned her right to a permanent tenancy. They would even put out greater quantities of acceptable foods so that she might not prowl so widely as to bring retribution on herself and family. Bob was promptly called and the decision carefully explained to him and his understanding family.

But the best intentions and well-laid plans of men often go to naught—at least where raccoons are involved. A few days later the lady phoned to say that Mother Raccoon and her entire litter had moved out—like the proverbial Arabs—one dark night. It was an affront to pride and affection, but it seemed to solve the problem of the man-across-the-fence and his grim threats.

Zsa-Zsa and her family

By the summer of 1964, the three raccoons, Zsa-Zsa, George, and Andy, which came as orphan babies in July 1962, were acting quite adult. Both George and Andy became romantically involved with Zsa-Zsa and at times fought rather bitterly over their attentions to her. We looked for indications of blessed events, but whenever we thought there were signs, we were disappointed.

On the morning of August 31, the animal keeper found the coati in the adjacent cage cleaning up the remains of something that looked suspiciously like a baby raccoon. Quick inspection of the raccoon cage revealed Zsa-Zsa to be in the process of giving birth to an offspring while George and Andy looked on in some puzzlement.

Zsa-Zsa was promptly transferred to a large wire cage kept in the loft of the feed house. This she accepted with good grace and by that noon had delivered two tiny but well-furred babies. She seemed quite content to lie there and nurse them.

138

Pirate, the raccoon, explores bedroom drawer.

Things went well for two or three days in the loft nursery. Then Zsa-Zsa began to resent such strict confinement and tackled the situation in typical raccoon fashion. That meant find the door catch and get out. This she did for two or three nights, having a grand time prowling the loft, so we realized she would have to be moved out into a regular cage.

We gave Zsa-Zsa a carrying box with wire mesh on the front and top so that her babies would have to remain in the nest unless she chose to carry them outside. This was placed with its solid back against the partition between her cage and the coyote's as this position gave viewers the best opportunity to see within.

Every morning the nest box was in a different position in the cage—even upside down with the babies spilled out on the cold concrete. There were other signs that the family was having bad nights. Zsa-Zsa was extremely nervous during the day too, but it took several days to discover the reason. We did suspect Missie, the coyote, but she had been such a fearful animal that it seemed unlikely that she would act the big-bad-wolf role.

Then one of the night visitors to the Junior Zoo observed the shy lady coyote sniffing and drooling at the raccoon's dividing mesh. Instead of trying to reach through and scratch this menacing neighbor, Zsa-Zsa was frantically trying to move her family as far as possible from the coyote.

Once provided with this information, we erected a low divider of opaque plastic material to block Missie's view of the raccoon family. With wire we attached the raccoon nest box firmly to the opposite side of the cage. These measures appeared to calm Zsa-Zsa, and she settled down to the routine of child care.

As the babes grew larger, opened their eyes, and became quite irresistible, some of us felt that Mother should share them with us for short periods. But Mother quite plainly didn't see it that way. A crisis came when repairs just had to be made in their cage. How to get into Zsa-Zsa's home was the question.

An opportunity came when the keeper managed to lock Zsa-Zsa in a carrying case and her babies in another. This meant a chance not only to fix her quarters, but to get acquainted with her children. Present at this time was a student helper, a college girl who had begged ever since the blessed event for a baby raccoon. This was the time we had been waiting for to get our hands on these precious infants and to photograph them. The helper was most willing to cooperate. While she fondled the twins, I snapped pictures. Zsa-Zsa, meanwhile, growled and stormed from her secure little case.

How to replace Zsa-Zsa in her cage—and more particularly how to restore her babies to her without getting clawed—was the next problem. It wasn't too hard to place the portable cage at the rear door and slip the mother back into her quarters. But we were still stuck with two little raccoons on the outside and their mother raging around on the inside.

Zsa-Zsa was distracted by presenting one child at the front of the cage while the other was quickly replaced through the back door. This didn't completely satisfy her, as the other baby continued to cry pitifully. But when she cuddled her baby for a few moments in the nest box, we opened the back door again and replaced the second child.

What about the maxim that you can't handle wild animal babies and restore them to their mother? Well, we had once again disproved that. We wouldn't say that the rule was worthless—just less applicable among zoo and pet animals.

After this we did handle the babies two or three times while Mother was begging handouts at the front of the cage. But it was always a touch-and-go business to get them back into their cage.

After six weeks, Zsa-Zsa began to wean her little ones and become less jealous of them. By late October we actually borrowed one baby for several pet shows.

Returning from a vacation in November, I found Zsa-Zsa had only one child with her. My staff had yielded to an urgent appeal from a top-level scientific mission for a young raccoon. A psychiatrist at the California Medical Center in San Francisco wanted a tame juvenile raccoon to study and relate its learning habits to those of human infants.

Zsa-Zsa appeared to accept fate, though for a time it was evident that she missed her other child and looked around for it. Soon she became much less solicitous of the remaining child as it began to imitate her habit of begging handouts at the front of the cage. In fact, she actually returned to moods of great affection when she greeted the keepers at cleaning and feeding times. She would clutch them and allow herself to be carried out to the front rail for introductions to visitors while her child remained in the cage. On other occasions she would wrestle and play-fight so violently with her offspring that onlookers would fear real harm to the baby. Once the child came up with a dangling toe joint which demanded an emergency operation. Soon after that we separated mother and child in adjoining cages as Zsa-Zsa showed signs of wanting to get back to the upper cage with her brothers, and we thought by this method we could someday make the complete separation.

Possum pranks

"No thank you, we just cannot take on any more possums.* We are overloaded with them," I said to this disturbed feminine voice over the phone as she told of finding young possums in her back yard.

"Oh no. That isn't why I called you. We divided the possum family with the neighbors, and all eight babies are eating fine. What I want to ask you is something else. A friend has been telling me about possums, and I've just got to ask someone who knows."

"Go right ahead," I said with a feeling of relief. It is always easier to give information than to have a box of unwanted orphans on your desk.

---

*Scientifically known as the Common or Virginia Opossum.

141

"Well," continued this voice with some hesitation, "this friend says they breed through their noses. Could such a thing be true?"

I choked momentarily before I could find my tongue to assure this gullible gal that nothing was farther from the facts about possums. Then I added that this was only one of many early legends connected with possums, and that the lady should visit our nature library and consult the literary masterpiece on the Virginia Opossum by Dr. Carl G. Hartman. The entire book is devoted to this marsupial and to the fantastic descriptions and yarns which built up a possum folklore in the American South.

Such imaginary traits and inventions by pseudo-naturalists are quite unnecessary to attract attention to this strange animal. A mammal with a marsupial pouch, a prehensile tail, and a habit of feigning death when suddenly attacked hardly needs any buildup.

It is North America's only marsupial, and it gives birth to several more young than its pouch with seven to thirteen teats can accomodate. When the twelve to twenty-five bee-size babies are born, it's a case of every infant for itself. Ordinarily only seven to ten make it and find teats to attach themselves to and cling to for

Possum babies prefer to cling to mother's fur, but may occasionally grasp her strong tail.

142

eight to ten weeks. These lucky survivors begin to hang out tail-first and then to venture out of mother's brooder-chamber when they have grown fur and opened their eyes. Soon they are munching any soft food that mother finds on her overnight foraging trips.

Possum babies are bareback riders when they grow too large and sensitive to remain in mother's pouch. Their tiny, tenacious front feet clutch mother's fur, while they practice new holds with their hind feet which have opposable "thumbs" like a human hand. Grasping or prehensile naked tails may occasionally seize the mother's huge tail for support as they begin to venture away from the female. But I have never seen a litter lined up and swinging from mother's tail, nor do young or old possums hang themselves at rest by the hour in such a position.

Rearing possum babies which have fallen from the pouch before their normal emergence stage is extremely difficult. Their tiny mouths are shaped to the teats, which become elongated and provide anchorage and tethering for the babes within the pouch. Nature has even provided their windpipe openings with a special lid or epiglottis that enables them to breathe and suckle simultaneously. If you must rescue a possum infant, find a doll nursing bottle with a long thin nipple and administer warmish milk very sparingly.

Emerged young of eight weeks of age or more are rather easily reared, starting them out with soft dog food, meat, egg, and fruit. They quickly become accustomed to handling. Occasionally, they may take playful nips at the fingers that feed them. They also make unexpected jumps from various positions and heights with no regard for consequences.

Playing possum

Don't expect your possum pets of any age to play dead for show. They rarely pull this stunt once they have been handled awhile and have been exposed to the neighborhood cats and dogs, though I have known newly-caught possums to display their feigning act during a junior zoo demonstration.

I am inclined to take sides with the zoologists who claim the possum's "playing dead" is the result of a traumatic shock over which the animal has no control. Dr. Hartman cites many other examples among birds, mammals, and reptiles where similar death feigning is observed. We ourselves induce blue-bellied lizards to do this by placing them on their backs and stroking their bellies. Because of the possum's limited intelligence, it seems doubtful that it would deliberately choose this type of defense.

Possums may not actually have nine lives, but I have sometimes been flabbergasted at demonstrations of recovery from serious wounds. One particular episode comes to mind.

"Paul, can you come up here and see what kind of an animal I just killed? It looked like an oversize rat, and I found it in the chicken house and gave it the pitchfork. It's in the garbage can now."

This SOS came by phone from John, a gardener friend. He knew horticulture from experience on three continents but had never become familiar with California's birds and beasts. John lived nearby so I was soon at his home, set on a quarter acre of garden and orchard. His chicken house was probably the last in the neighborhood.

John led me down the path to a garbage can that stood beside the chicken coop. He lifted the lid of the can and started to reach for the animal's carcass. Growling and chomping its formidable jaws, a big male possum came crawling out of that can, jumped to the ground, and started for safer places.

John was too paralyzed to do much about it. Fortunately, there was a spade nearby, and I made sure the possum's remaining eight lives were extinguished. He couldn't have lived too long after John's pitchfork attack.

The common opossum has really taken over the state of California. It was brought from the East and South and planted in several California localities around the turn of the century. Like the Eastern fox squirrel, which arrived by transplants about the same era, the possum cast its lot with man and man's abundant food supplies. There the comparisons must end.

Possums soon moved into towns. Basements, garages, even culverts offered snug homes. Many a frantic summons have we answered, and many a possum have we removed from someone's garage, storage shed, or basement. Such responses were the occasions when we needed a female with family for the Junior Zoo. At other times, the city pound has met our possum needs.

Everyone loves Bambi

Once you raise a baby deer—known as a fawn—you're hooked. I guess it is like a home that accepts human waifs and

144

rears them with some measure of success. I never made a study of such places or their foster parents, but I suspect they receive many more offers of orphans than they can accept. That has been the history of the Oakland Park naturalists, the Children's Fairyland staff, and a few other naturalists I know where fawns are concerned.

Billy Blacktail was first announced by a long distance call from a game warden. The orphan was less than a week old—could he bring it to Lakeside Park? He said he would rather entrust it to us than to anyone else he knew, as a sort of clincher to his appeal.

I broke the glad news at home that evening. "Another fawn!" exclaimed my spouse and special assistant for animal orphans. "You'll have to fix the garage doors and the gate across the driveway. Remember how your son followed that last one out of the driveway and down the street."

Before noon the next day the warden left his charge at the Natural Science Center. The limp, brown, spotted creature collapsed and was not the most promising baby. Spindly legs hung out in all directions as we picked it up for examination. Big, limpid brown eyes occupied much of a head that was far out of proportion to a thin body with starkly prominent ribs.

The warden and his family had fed the orphan, but nobody knew how many meals he had missed before he was found and brought to the warden. A half-wild dog pack had crippled the doe, its mother.

We brought out the nursing bottle, a nipple, and a can of evaporated milk. We would start the baby on the standard half-and-half formula. Later we would add a little Karo syrup or make other formula changes as circumstances indicated. Goat's milk, we later found, was excellent.

Billy Blacktail, as we decided to call him, was not prepared to accept us as foster parents—at least not without a protest. But we had been through this little game before. It's a struggle between gnawing hunger and an inherent fear of man. We held our fawn firmly, gently forced the nipple between his lips and waited. A little of the lukewarm milk trickled down his throat. This felt too good to resist. He began to suck on the nipple.

Billy could actually get to his feet and stand, even if a bit wobbly. We carried him outdoors and placed him in a corner of the big duck roundup cage in the middle of the duck feeding yard where other fawns had grown up in this spacious enclosure.

Some of the regular habitués of the duck feeding yard could never accept such an intrusion by a new four-legged animal without close examination and vociferous comments. The big Toulouse geese and the Chinese geese, in particular, gathered around the cage as soon as Billy stood up. Their sonorous blasts must have been a frightening experience for the fawn. But in a few days he would ignore them, and they would accept him as one of the Park Family.

Animal babies do not adjust to eight-hour working days, any more than do human infants. Ask any zoo director's wife or family. At Center closing time Billy had to be placed in a lightweight dog-carrying case and loaded into the family car to go home with me.

Privacy and quiet evenings are not possible with fawns or other wild babies in one's house or yard. We knew what to expect. But this time we tried to smuggle the new deer child into our home before the news got out. He obviously needed a day or two to get acquainted with the family and garden before the neighborhood children heard about him.

Billy seemed to appreciate his first feeding in the comparative quiet of the garden. Jimmy, our lively young son, didn't appear to worry him very much—in fact, a mutual attraction soon developed between them. Many animal young are more attracted to human children, and of course the reverse is even more obvious, and yet little boys and girls may need considerable training to properly care for young animals.

We did have some problems with this orphan. Billy showed the common diarrhea symptoms after just a few bottles. We eliminated the Karo syrup for awhile and a few days later changed his formula to plain homogenized milk with a tablespoon of baby cereal added to each bottle. By the second day he was taking five eight-ounce bottles daily, spaced at about three-hour intervals from 7 a.m. to 9 p.m. He weighed in at nearly six pounds and stood fourteen inches high at the shoulder.

I wanted to avoid getting Billy imprinted to me—as the animal behaviorists say. I didn't want him to regard me as his one and only foster parent. But this tendency was extremely difficult to avoid, although the fawn was accepting his bottle from my wife, son, several neighborhood children, and some of the staff and junior volunteers at the Park. Still, he bleated when within range of my voice and wanted to follow me, regardless of where the way might lead.

146

A friend was purposely asked to bring along his small dog when he came to see the fawn. Neither fawn nor dog showed much interest in each other. Another time a four-foot-long gopher snake was released in front of Billy. This animal, too, drew little interest from the fawn after an initial sniff or two. Could it be that a doe's reactions or warnings are necessary to implant a fear of potential enemies?

Billy's other instincts appeared to be developing nicely. Many kinds of flowers and leaves were delicately nibbled. English ivy and petunias seemed to draw the most return trips for tasting. Increasing amounts of plain soil were eaten by Billy, this, we understand, for a "stomach culture" which must include certain bacteria. The first time I observed him munching garden soil, I went into a panic and seized the poor animal to determine if he had been including snail pellets. If he had, they didn't bother him at all. I quickly cleaned up the rest of the pellets.

Billy would suddenly disappear after a meal and romp in the garden. Nature told him to hide out somewhere and digest his

Everyone is a friend to Becky.

food—and hide he did most effectively. This led to a tantalizing game of hide and seek when it was time to confine him to the garage for the night.

At the end of his fifth week, the fawn weighed 15 pounds and stood 18 inches high at the shoulder. He had accepted a collar and leash. At least, he would go along obediently with the leash when hungry or in a playful mood. But he no longer accepted confinement to that dog-carrying case without a protest. When it was loaded in the back of the station wagon, he would flail around with his little hoofs and the light case would dance a bit. This was distracting not only to my driving but to some drivers who pulled up behind at stop signals.

A fawn in Fairyland

The time of all-night separation from the family had arrived. I took the big step of leaving him at Fairyland one evening, hoping that a last bottle after closing time would hold him overnight. Billy must have sensed that something was wrong when twilight found him in the Fairyland holding pen instead of our garden. He refused his early evening bottle from the night custodian and continued bleating loudly and plaintively. The man was worried and stopped the ranger on patrol.

"Don't worry, I'll call Covel," volunteered the ranger. This was the customary solution for any overnight problems involving animals.

At Fairyland I warmed the bottle and I formally introduced the night man and the ranger to Billy. He seemed to get the message, took the bottle with some reluctance from both these strangers, and finally quieted down. That was the only night Billy gave us any trouble. The ranger fed him each night for several weeks.

Billy couldn't be turned over completely to Fairyland. It was late June and hundreds of boys and girls attending day camps expected to see the park naturalists and their wild animal pets, and no such pet could draw a more enthusiastic welcome than a Bambi. Poor Billy had to endure more rides in the dog-carrying case two or three days each week, packed in among a possum, skunk, snakes, and others of "the cast" as we made the rounds of the day camps.

Sometimes it would be a nature show on a city playground instead of one of the campsites framed in wooded hills. At such

148

a place, disrupting sounds of passing traffic and nearby ball games would distract the deer's attention. Loose dogs are always a problem when animal shows are given out-of-doors in urban settings. One day a big German shepherd came rushing through the surrounding circle of children during a playground performance. He had spotted Billy and with terrifying barks made straight for him. The fawn reared back and struck out in the direction of the shepherd with his forefeet. This took the dog by surprise. Someone collared the dog and led him away. I brought out the nursing bottle, and the show went on. Here we had a seven-week-old buck who wouldn't give up the bottle but could put up a fight on occasion!

Billy Blacktail rode the day-camp circuit well into his third month. From habit he would still take the bottle, but it was now comfort and not a necessity. He was dining regularly on dry alfalfa, oats, and sundry snacks. Goats and their kids were his regular companions at Fairyland. His spots were fading, and his tiny incisors and molars were grinding popcorn and sample bits of paper and cloth.

Finally this orphan became completely a Fairyland resident in the goat corral. Thousands of visitors of all ages met and loved this overgrown baby. When bottle feeding for the goat kids was announced, he would trot up to the rail and try to push the kids aside in greedy attempts to get something he no longer needed.

By the following year both Billy's size and sex rendered him unsuitable for Fairyland. He might have been turned loose in the hill parks to grow fat and bold on wild or garden plants, but the next fall, when his sex glands and his neck swelled, he might become dangerous. After all, he had become a "people's deer" and might not realize he should take to the woods and find himself a cute doe.

Fate intervened kindly for us and for Billy. A suburban children's zoo offered to take him for their spacious deer corral. They came for him one quiet weekday in November. I didn't go over to watch him coaxed into their truck. After all, he had been part of our family, and we've had enough heartbreaks that we couldn't avoid.

Lucy and her family

Among all the orphan fawns that have romped in our garden and eventually "graduated" from the Naturalists' and Fairyland kindergarten, Lucy was by far the most out-standing.

Lucy was offered a home in the unfenced Nature Area of Tilden Regional Park, located beyond the hill residential section of Berkeley. Other wild deer became half tame, grazed, and browsed in this semi-wild park, and it was hoped Lucy would associate with both her kind and with people, and remain within the boundaries.

Lucy became a husky doe by her first spring-summer at the Nature Area. She had plenty of temptations to roam the range with the wild deer, but she entertained other ideas. She felt herself to be part of "the staff." Weekends and early evenings she greeted each picnic party and graciously accepted handouts. But it was on the school days that she distinguished herself by special services.

As each bus load of eager children came into the Nature Area, Lucy greeted them and stood by patiently while they got their briefing. When the group took the conducted walk along the nature trail, Lucy fell in line, usually toward the rear, and stayed with the class until every child who wished could pet her. She didn't expect any donation—this was part of her regular job.

That fall Lucy disappeared for short periods until early one morning one of the naturalists saw Lucy in company with a handsome buck. Lucy trotted a few steps toward her human friend; the buck snorted and took off up the hillside.

Lucy returned to the Nature Area and resumed some of her customary duties, but she took frequent absences without leave. Toward spring it became obvious that her girlish figure was undergoing changes. Lucy was an expectant mother!

About the first of May, the doe dropped out of sight for a few weeks. An atmosphere of tense expectation formed around the Nature Area headquarters. The naturalists, the secretary-receptionist, and regular visitors made friendly wagers on when Lucy would return with her child.

And there she was, very proud and confident, early one morning when the staff came to work. Josh Barkin, Resident Naturalist, and his wife Pearl were the first to greet her and her fawn, right at their back door.

The fawn was still a little wobbly and neither fawn nor mother wanted humans handling it right away. When the fawn

Becky Fawn poses with friend.

wanted to nurse, Lucy led it up into the tall grass. She would leave it there to nap while she returned to graze a bit on the lush lawn.

Lucy reared her first fawn to become a "staff deer," although it never acquired its mother's complete familiarity with visitors. The next spring Lucy startled everyone by bringing in twin fawns. This she repeated twice during her long residence at Tilden. Twins do occur in about one fourth of the births among the California mule and black-tailed deer, according to Dr. Lloyd Ingles in his excellent volume, "Mammals of California." Lucy did better.

Lucy might have lived to a ripe old deer age at Tilden Park except for an accident in the early summer of her sixth year. No one knew exactly how it happened, but there she was one morning dragging a broken leg.

As she was also large with another fawn, Lucy was in a serious condition.

Carefully and gently Lucy was picked up and placed in the back of a van. A veterinarian was called, and he promised to do what he could. He put on an ambulatory cast, but said it might not work for such an active animal. Besides, she would probably give birth to her offspring in a few weeks.

Lucy did return to Tilden Park with her "walking cast." She presented rather a pitiful figure as she limped around the Nature Area. Shortly afterward her fawn came into the world. She nursed it faithfully and pretty soon it was gamboling about its mother who was finding the going rougher and rougher with that funny plaster leg.

By mid-summer it became evident that Lucy wouldn't make it. Her leg was not healing. She could hardly rise from the ground to follow her lively child. Sadly the naturalist staff decided to call the kindly doctor to put Lucy out of her misery.

But Lucy lived on in the Nature Area, and in other regional parks.* Naturalist Josh Barkin and his wife, Pearl, have included her in the animal cast of an educational puppet show, together with Racky Raccoon, Reddy Redwing, and other neighbors she knew so well.

*The Interpretive Division of the East Bay Regional Park system, which could claim only one part-time naturalist in 1947, when the Oakland program was launched, has grown to a force of fifteen full-time interpreters, supported by student aides, secretary-receptionists and an exhibits laboratory! This force operates visitors' centers and nature walks in a vast park network in two counties.

Animal Immigrants in the City

Assistant Naturalist Lionel Kett, grinning triumphantly, came bursting into the Center carrying an aluminum animal carrying case. Loud, plaintive chirps and a broad bristly muzzle in the door grill of the case brought exclamations of surprise and pleasure from me. The little guest was an otter—the first such mammal ever brought to the Duck Pond. And it appeared to be young and friendly. Mr. Kett had received a call late the previous evening from the county animal shelter asking if we wanted this strange creature they had found wandering on a suburban street. He said we did and had retrieved the otter from amid the cages of howling, barking, and whining dogs at the shelter.

A young otter is always greeted with rejoicing at the average zoo. But otters need water, and water we didn't have within an otter-proof enclosure. We couldn't expect this lively animal to

153

live around the Duck Island pools and catch its fish in the
salty lake.

This prize mammal was given the run of the office and was
busy examining every nook, cranny, and low shelf it could reach.
We determined the otter was a female and named her "Susie."
Susie was a cuddler and kisser as long as you didn't hold her too
tight or too long.

It was all too plain that we couldn't quickly construct a
proper otter pool within one of the small cages. We had once tried
to keep a muskrat with a sink for his cage swims, and it didn't
work. No, I'd have to come up with a better home for Susie, and
I did want to keep her within the park pet family.

Why not the Robinson Crusoe set at Children's Fairyland?
It had a high wall, a moat, and an island. Monkeys of various
species, macaws, and parrots, ducks, alligators, and turtles had all
inhabited this enclosure over the years. True, many of the monkeys and birds had escaped after becoming familiar with their
surroundings, but there had been surprisingly little conflict among
such different denizens. Mr. Kett muttered something about
giving up such a valuable animal to a gardener's care, and I thought
the keeper was going to shed a tear or two. But I insisted that
Susie should be tried out at Fairyland—that is, if they would
accept her.

Susie Otter had different ideas when we asked her to step
back into the carrying case. She liked our building, had accepted
a quickly thawed piece of fish in a bowl of water, and apparently
was willing to stay awhile. A little forceful persuasion brought
a show of teeth and angry chirps from Susie. She also demonstrated an uncanny ability to slither between our grasping hands,
feet, even a catch net. Her ridiculously short legs propelled her
at an amazing speed in a funny, undulating movement.

Susie was cornered and forced into her carrying case. Her
protests were almost ear-splitting as I carried her out of the Center
and to the truck headed for Fairyland. A small source of comfort
to me was that by then the staff had realized this otter was no
lap pet and might have become quite a problem confined in a
small space.

Getting Susie accepted at Fairyland was no problem once
Director Charlotte Rowe saw her impish face and heard her piteous
calls. She summoned the head gardener to help get Susie installed
in the Robinson Crusoe set.

We threw the gangplank across to Crusoe's Island and carried Susie over, case and all. Then we opened the door. Out she bounded with eager chirps. Round and round the little concrete island she went, and up and down on the lower beams supporting Crusoe's watchtower. The gold and scarlet macaw screamed from overhead, and the big spider monkey chattered, but they didn't faze Susie. She did come back frequently to climb on my knee and be petted. Apparently I was completely forgiven for my part in capturing her over at the Center.

Susie obviously needed a bath and didn't seem inclined to take one. We tried various devices to get her into the shallow waters of the moat where the tame ducks had bunched up for protection from this suspicious intruder. Finally I grabbed Susie by her long, flattened tail and threw her into the moat. With a rather frantic dog-paddle stroke, she quickly returned to the island and began a vigorous shaking and rubbing against the wooden beams to dry her fur. Then we realized her underfur and long guard hairs lacked natural waterproofing. The truth was — Susie had never been exposed to deep water or taught to swim.

Why wouldn't an otter be born with waterproofed fur? The answer, I believe, is that while Susie wore the right type of fur, it lacked the proper nourishment and stimulation. We suspected the youngster had been reared indoors and never forced to enter water as it would have by a natural mother. If her former owners had reared her on dog or cat food instead of fish, some of the essential oils may have been lacking.

Susie goes exploring

Susie soon won the hearts of the entire Fairyland staff, including the gardeners who would have to "walk the gangplank" to Crusoe's Island an extra trip or two with fish and a little canned dog food. She would squeal piteously when the first gardener appeared each morning. Even after a substantial breakfast, she would continue to look for human company, which wasn't too plentiful on weekdays as the winter season drew on.

For a sleeping den, a small box had been placed at the center of the island under Crusoe's Watchtower. Straw was provided for bedding, but Susie took this for play material and scattered it far and wide. A burlap sack fared no better. Yet everybody felt sorry when the otter curled up on a bare floor in the box. Then someone thought of Crusoe's Treasure Chest. This decorative piece was placed off the concrete on the lower rungs of the Watch-tower. The lid was propped up and a narrow board ladder set beside it.

Within minutes, curious Susie had investigated this alluring cavity. All day she ran back and forth between the chest and ground level. A bed of straw had been added to the chest. By late afternoon she had adopted this as her new sleeping chamber.

A day or two later, the gardener was greeted with particularly frantic chirps when he approached the Crusoe set and called Susie. Then he noticed the propped lid of the chest had been knocked closed. Susie was trapped and had worked up quite a panic. When freed, she slobbered profuse kisses and climbed all over her rescuer. To avoid repetition of such a mishap, a small hole was sawed in the bottom of the Treasure Chest for Susie's regular use. The lid was then only used for cleaning purposes.

Weekly pool cleaning and island scrubbing was Susie's special day of frolic. On this day the gardener remained inside the Robin-son Crusoe Set for two or three hours. He would start by draining the moat. As the water lowered, Susie got bolder, chased the strand-ed ducks a bit and sniffed at the turtles. But she never hurt a one.

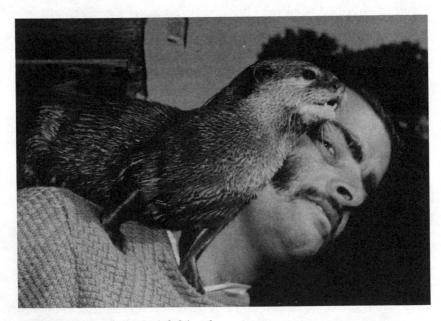

Susie Otter and a special friend.

In the midst of pool scrubbing one day, the gardener realized that Susie hadn't been sniffing around his boots and chirping for love and kisses. Then he heard chirps from outside the Crusoe set. Susie was on a tour of Fairyland. And what an excursion she was having! The two Toulouse geese had spotted this suspicious intruder and were adding their cacaphonous protests to the excitement.

Susie was recaptured with the aid of a fish or two. So many strange scenes and animals had proved a bit tiring and bewildering to the little fugitive. It took awhile to discover the otter's escape route. It was the concrete planter in the middle of the moat from which she could leap to the outer rim. But she would only use this trick when the moat had been emptied.

About a year after Susie's arrival, a distress call from Fairyland broke the news that Susie was missing at morning muster. Then reports of Susie's whereabouts began to come in. Citizens had seen her loping along the edge of the lake, going through the show gardens, drinking from a fountain, and so on. One or two observers had called gardeners, and they had come within feet of the otter which chirped a friendly greeting and then took off at high speed.

It was inevitable that Susie would sooner or later reach the Duck Pond. This wouldn't be too great a disaster—only a major disturbance. Susie wasn't likely to kill even a pigeon, but the birds didn't know that.

Three bus loads of school children were present in the Duck Pond when it happened. Mr. Kett and I had already given them the indoor orientation and introductions, and we were in the midst of the outside tour. Everything was proceeding in an orderly fashion.

An otter in birdland

The scene changed to bedlam. Tame pigeons rose with a clatter of wings. Mallard ducks, Canada geese, gray Toulouse and white Chinese geese all headed for the lake—their instinctive reaction in times of danger. The chorus of quacks and goose voices in many keys was shattering, particularly for those urban children who had never before witnessed a mass upheaval of waterfowl. Some of the kids shielded their heads with their arms in fear that this was a demonstration against them.

The cause of this panic was little Susie nonchalantly loping across the feeding area to the lower beach. She didn't appear to be pursuing any particular bird, but every duck, goose, swan, and mudhen regarded this strange creature as a mortal enemy.

The animal keeper got a net. Several bystanders hastened to help in the otter's capture. Mr. Kett and I tried to explain why the birds panicked, and that Susie Otter was quite harmless to everybody.

Susie, having explored the feeding area and the beach and finding all those strange feathered creatures so unfriendly, started back across the park. The keeper and his posse cornered her, but the otter slipped right through the bird net they had thrown over her.

At this point, Robert, the Fairyland gardener who was her special friend and confidant, was called. He promised to come immediately.

Susie was down at the water's edge when Robert and his helper arrived. A hostile semicircle of waterfowl floated just off shore, noisily protesting her presence, while Susie chirped back at them in a friendly way. Only the whistling swans and the white pelicans actually threatened to charge ashore and take on the intruder.

Robert decided on the "soft sell" in capturing his pet. He brought along only a carrying case and a supply of small fish — no nets and no heavy handling gloves. We chided him for his excessive confidence in such methods, but he just kneeled at the water's edge and held out fish. Susie splashed out into the shallows and turned around to survey the situation.

The class tours were over, but the children and teachers stood along the railing at the lake overlook and shouted encouragement to us and some to the otter.

Robert tossed out a fish which Susie deftly caught and chewed. He tossed a second and a third, each time a little closer to himself and to the open case beside him. The otter was hungry after her escapade and continued to accept and eat the fish until she was right beside Robert. Then he dropped the last fish and reached for her. With a sharp, annoyed chirp, she bared her teeth, slipped out of his hands, and took off for Duck Island. Three swans and a couple of pelicans rushed to surround her, the swans ready to strike with their powerful wings. A chorus of alarm arose from the gallery of spectators. Susie was no longer interested in fish bait and was determined to reach Duck Island if she could only dodge those funny birds.

Susie made it to Duck Island One. Robert asked for the keys to the rowboat, but he and his helper were back within the hour. After a short chase around the island, Susie had found an impenetrable brush pile and had curled up and gone to sleep. Now they would bait a live trap with fish and await her pleasure.

Late that afternoon, she was still napping and merely yawned at her pursuers when they peeked in on her. But the next morning Susie was in the live trap. She was chirping furiously at her inflexible jailer. The fish bait had been eaten to the last scale.

Susie greeted her home quarters with evident relief and pleasure and stayed there for the rest of her life. The episode seemed to have taught her the advantages of swimming, for after that, she leaped readily into the lagoon waters surrounding her little island.

Susie puzzled us by ceasing to grow. The American river otter reaches four feet or more in length, while this animal didn't exceed twenty-two inches. Finally a zoo man identified Susie as a small-clawed otter of southern Asia.

Prairie dogs far from home

Park and playland designers have a habit of creating imaginative, but sometimes impractical, settings for exotic or hard-to-get animals. The operators or directors of these places then encounter perplexing problems when it comes time to animate these beautiful sets. That's what happened when we began to look for prairie dogs to enliven the Ten Little Indians set designed for Children's Fairyland.

The major zoos in California that were permitted to import and display these vanishing Americans didn't care to share any specimens with us. But our enterprising superintendent of parks located a protected prairie dog colony at Lubbock, Texas. Yes, those big-handed Texans would ship some. Then the California Department of Agriculture said that prairie dogs were on the banned list and relented on condition that only males be sent and that they be neutered immediately.

Weeks passed and then word came that it was too late in the season to trap the "dogs." Some more time elapsed and news came that sixteen prairie dogs were en route via United Air Freight. It was understood that eight of them would be sent to the Sacramento Zoo whose director, Hank Spencer, had helped persuade the Department of Agriculture to grant the permit.

At the Oakland Airport, I found a crate of lively "dogs" which couldn't be counted or sexed due to the abundant loose sacking they hid in. I asked the freight clerk if we should notify any officials of their arrival. Upon being advised we need not do so, I took them directly to Fairyland. Personnel from the Sacramento Zoo came down promptly to pick up their eight "dogs."

The following week, eight prairie dogs were living happily on the sand-and-cactus set enclosed by a three-foot wall. They already had a burrow system well underway. Then the storm struck. The local agricultural commissioner hadn't yet been notified, but read the newspaper story of the arrival of the prairie dogs. He was extremely agitated (to put it mildly) and demanded all the animals be caught, inspected, all males neutered, and any and all females immediately destroyed. We captured the eight "dogs" and found there were *six females!*

After some consultation, we were allowed to keep all of the "dogs" provided they were neutered by a veterinarian. I never did learn the sex of the "dogs" that went to the Sacramento Zoo.

The prairie dog colony in Children's Fairyland proved to be one of the star attractions from late spring through early fall. These lively rodents shared the cactus and succulent garden with some desert tortoise. Each fall after these animals retired into hibernation, the tortoises within the little stucco house and the "dogs" into their underground burrows, the gardeners smoothed the hills and caved-in tunnels and replanted the topsy-turvy succulents into a semblance of landscaped design. Then, by the middle of the next season's activities, the entire set came to resemble Topsy-Turvy Land again.

There had been escapes from the Fairyland colony, but they were promptly trapped and returned. In the social order of this colony, there was one which became the "bottom dog on the totem pole." She was removed for her own security and was eventually brought to the Junior Zoo at the Duck Feeding area, where she lived in a small wire cage and played to a daily audience by spinning a wheel and getting tidbits from visitors in return for her act.

Once in awhile this contented "dog" did manage to escape from her small cage, but she merely threw up a few mounds nearby in the larger enclosure and was easily caught in a live trap and returned to her cage. When fresh "diggings" outside her cage appeared, we concluded she was out again.

160

Once when fresh mounds were seen, an observer reported that "doggie" was still in her own cage and that a second prairie dog had been seen in the mouth of the new burrow. A call to Fairyland confirmed that one of the colony had disappeared a few days before. Some sense had guided this new escapee about a quarter of a mile to the Duck Pond where she had then to dig through a rat hole to reach proximity to her friend.

No less than three types and sizes of live traps were set around her principal burrow. It soon became evident that she didn't plan to be trapped. A week later the traps were still unsprung. In fact the runaway "dog" hadn't even been seen for several days.

Two weeks later, a gardener from across the lake called, "Bring a live trap. We've got what looks like a prairie dog digging under the tool house."

Here was a real puzzler. In order to arrive at this area on the downtown side of Lake Merritt, the little rodent had to make her way along at least a mile of shoreline, or else she managed to swim two hundred yards across the intervening arm of the lake.

To conclude: our heroine soon vanished from the vicinity across the lake. Could her remarkable nose or instinct have guided her eastward across freeways, cities, and mountains toward her former home in Texas? Well, not really, but this wandering "doggie" did know how to get around.

An illegal immigrant

A friend in the Department of Fish and Game telephoned about an urgent and confidential case. It all began with a little Mexican which was smuggled into the U.S.A. by Miss Anne, a Berkeley girl, who saw and fell in love with this coati-mundi in a Mexican marketplace and decided to bring it home. She said the natives were talking about eating this poor animal. It just had to be rescued, and Miss Anne never thought about possible quarantine regulations or any other obstacles in raising such a pet in a small apartment in the city.

If it hadn't been for a write-up complete with a photograph turned in by a local reporter, Miss Anne and "Frances" might have enjoyed a long happy life together. But the appealing story came to the attention of concerned parties in the Department of Fish and Game which, together with the State Department of Agriculture, controls animal importations.

The Fish and Game warden, a humane and understanding chap, had been delegated to accompany a Department of Agriculture official to convey to Miss Anne the unwelcome news that she must give up her pet.

A home in the Junior Zoo at Lakeside Park would be just the spot for this little tamale, Frances. Her mistress could visit her as often as she wished, and meanwhile, she would be enjoyed by a passing parade of visitors. If we could agree to accept this fugitive, the Department of Fish and Game and the sovereign state of California would be eternally grateful.

What else could we do? We had once had a coati-mundi which was given to us when half grown and remained quite a pet until he reached maturity and began to use his claws and teeth too promiscuously. Besides, coatis are southern Arizona residents which may someday reach California by their own volition, so we could display them as "southwestern animals." In the end we agreed to give a home to Frances if the warden and the other official could get possession of this contraband beast.

Late that afternoon the two heroes arrived with a carrying case which we knew contained Frances as she was scratching and squealing in protest. The warden was visibly shaken from his experience too. It wasn't that Frances herself gave them so much trouble, but rather her mistress. There had been quite a scene— just like tearing a child from its mother's bosom. And we took it that the warden hadn't been trained to deal with hysterical women.

Frances, the pawn in this struggle between the law and Miss Anne, had to remain overnight in the carrying case while we

prepared an outdoor cage. It was agreed that we should not call in the gentlemen of the press. The two men left for their offices across the bay, obviously much relieved now that this controversial animal had been placed in the hands of a neutral party.

Trouble broke out early the next morning when we tried to persuade Frances, which had been given temporary freedom of our office, to re-enter her carrying case for the short transfer to the junior zoo cage. This six-month-old coati had a temper and knew how to use its teeth. It was necessary to wear heavy gloves to deal with this tough little rascal. And when she was put in the six-foot-wide cage, she really hit the roof!

The power of the press

The local press telephoned for our version of the Frances episode. It seemed that Miss Anne had recovered from her shock and alerted certain sympathetic persons who, in turn, had called on the power of the press. This was a great human interest story, and a chance to needle certain state officials. Frances was fast turning into a "cause célèbre." Miss Anne would be down to visit her pet later in the day, and we had a date with the news photographer whenever she appeared.

More calls followed. The Department of Fish and Game gentlemen were becoming shaken again over this big build-up in the press. The director himself was calling from Sacramento to inquire about Frances' new home and if she were quite secure there. Since the new cages hadn't been designed manproof, we were beginning to wonder ourselves.

That afternoon Miss Anne, looking forlorn and tearful, appeared. We just had to admit her to the "behind the cages" space so that she might slip special tidbits to Frances and whisper endearing phrases without interference from the passing public. The reporter and photographer arrived, and we opened the cage door to let Miss Anne slip on a leash and pose Frances on her neck. Otherwise we might have been portrayed as the pitiless jailers. When we left that evening, Miss Anne was still clinging to Frances' cage, and all of us were getting a bit shaken by the business.

A slight nip of a visitor's finger next day served notice that Frances' cage would have to be lined with smaller mesh. The animal keepers also served notice that Frances wouldn't sit in a corner while they cleaned and serviced her quarters. This posed another problem as we couldn't have her jump out and run around town.

163

Then our Fish and Game friends dropped by with a newspaper story which disclosed that Frances' case had been brought to the governor's attention. The governor in his holiday munificence had expressed the hope that Frances might be "paroled to her protector for the Christmas holidays."

Miss Anne had travel plans for the holidays so we and the Department of Fish and Game were spared the agony of turning Frances back into her custody and then reclaiming her a few days later. As it was, we were busy enough answering the public's questions about Frances' fate.

Meanwhile Fish and Game had begun seeking another home for Frances, a home where this high-strung animal might have more constant company and attention. And so it was that the Josephine Randall Junior Museum in San Francisco offered Frances a home with another coati-mundi which already lived in their junior zoo. There Miss Anne would be welcome to visit often and stay as long as she liked.

This was indeed welcome news and an easy way of getting rid of an animal that might cause us even greater grief if she should escape, become ill, or be harmed in any way. The state official sounded so embarrassed at suggesting this new shift that we took the cue and pretended to agree to the arrangement only after the proper ifs, ands, and buts.

The next day, the warden came with a carrying case for Frances' next transfer. We couldn't maintain this attitude of reluctance to part with Frances—not with straight faces—so we broke down and thanked the warden for relieving us of this VIP Critter.

Monkey business at Fairyland

Among the many Fairyland animal performers who grew weary of the routine and confinement of the Robinson Crusoe set were five little squirrel monkeys. One of the monkeys tried a leap to a bush overhanging the narrow lagoon and made it.

That lucky leap meant freedom for all. Monkey number one was easily chased back the same day, but the next day number two joined him in a happy exploration of Fairyland and vicinity. They didn't annoy visitors. In fact, they were most circumspect in their behavior. But just about everyone who saw them capering around in the oaks was sure they should not be there and promptly reported it. Various staff members had to drop other duties and chase the little devils to pacify the public. But the squirrel

The animals' good Samaritan with squirrel monkeys outside Children's Fairyland.

monkeys became ever more difficult to catch. To make matters as bad as possible, by the end of that week all five were out enjoying this wondrous, new-found freedom. They would go back to their home on Robinson Crusoe Island at night for food and warm shelter, but no device could keep them there.

Pursuit and recapture soon became futile. The staff decided that visitors would have to be told that these little scamps belonged outside of any set, that they were harmless, and that they wouldn't leave Fairyland.

And so the squirrel monkeys lived happily in and around Fairyland the rest of that season. But when winter closing came and most of the other mammals and birds were sent to other homes, the monkeys became lonely. They took to exploring Lakeside Park farther and farther from the boundaries of Fairyland. Their forays occasionally took them to the lawn bowling greens where they found friendly citizens to dole out snacks and talk softly to them.

But the uninitiated Lakeside Park patrons reacted differently to these "swingers in the trees." Worried citizens, small boys and girls jubilant with their discovery, parents afraid for their offspring— all came trooping to the Science Center to report the runaways.

One fine morning, the head nurseryman telephoned in a state of panic, "Come and catch your monkeys. They're wrecking the camellia garden."

The squirrel monkeys were having a ball in the garden. The rascals were tasting flower after flower, then gleefully throwing the petals to the winds!

One nurseryman had set a live trap, but more help was needed— more traps, the animal keepers, and the naturalists with the nets. The monkeys had finally fled the camellias for safer perches in the nearby oaks from which they were taunting their pursuers.

Past experience with monkeys told us the pursuit was now useless, but we told the nurserymen that we would send up the nets and traps. It seemed they had managed to live-trap one of the little blighters, and they hoped his squeals for help would lure down his companions.

An hour later, a more imperative call came. The monkeys were still there waiting to swoop down on the camellias, and the nurserymen wanted us to do something right away. We did not have any special monkey-catching talents, we replied, but we could do one thing if the monkeys couldn't be caught or chased away. We would bring a small-bore vermin-control shotgun and put a quick, painless end to the whole monkey problem.

This offer brought the results we expected. The head nurseryman was a devout sportsman. At least three of his crew were more or less ardent nature lovers, with one of them likely to all but crack up over any violence or threat of violence toward a "park pet."

This ended further demands for our services. Later I checked with the head gardener at Fairyland about their camellias and the monkeys. "Oh, the monkeys have been tasting and eating some camellias for years, but they just don't eat enough to matter much." We concluded that the raid on the main camellia garden was just a spree by these simians with small-boy behavior habits, and we hoped it wouldn't happen again.

166

Survival Hike —
Babes in the Woods

I never dared use the title "Survival Hike" for the many nature walks, hikes, prowls, or discovery hikes I led in the Oakland Hills. Survival hikes are important wilderness endurance tests for some armed forces teams and advanced Boy Scout achievements where the participants are dropped off at remote points provided only with knives, fish lines, matches, compasses, and the clothes on their backs and hopefully picked up days later at a prescribed rendezvous. The average urban citizen, nature lover or not, would have been wary about responding with the children to such an invitation.

So I chose this chapter title a bit facetiously, even though on these "urban wilderness" explorations we did get acquainted with many excellent wild foods which are worth gathering as supplements to store-bought items and might even contribute to human survival in the event of a major emergency with resultant cut-offs of fresh produce. But I had in mind also the considerable array of hangups, aversions, and ignorance which had to be overcome and cured to enable city folks to enjoy and profit from an adventure of tasting, feeling, and smelling in the woods! I'm sure that at the end of two or three hours of such exposure some did have a feeling of survival!

167

To be sure, some tempting, promising titles were invented to lure our city friends to the hills. "A Raccoon Ramble with the Naturalist," or "Spring Discoveries in the Redwoods," the Naturalist Bulletin might read. These titles give the leader a lot of latitude.

We knew some of those who responded to these invitations to come hiking expected to meet some exciting animals face to face, such as a curious raccoon rambling beside the creek, a doe posing with her fawn, or a red-tailed hawk swooping to snatch a brush rabbit.

We had seen these things, but we couldn't schedule them so we had a few other surprises lined up along the trail. "Adventures of the Senses," we might term them. This was our chance to make botany meaningful, to make even the humble plants underfoot and some wayside weeds come alive. Since elaborate wilderness survival courses are part of the training for some groups, why not begin close to home where we might have to survive someday?

Chances are that the first wayside plant that offers a green salad snack is miner's lettuce or Indian lettuce. This purslane family member has a unique round leaf surrounding a delicate flowering stem. It is delicious when the morning dew is on it—at least to raw food addicts and any surviving California Indians who may still use it. But the Indians had to smear ants on this and other wild greens to give them flavor.

Wild medicines are nearby too. For example, the good herb or yerba buena of the Spanish-Californian pioneers is likely to be seen. The leader carefully picks up one of the creeping stems, pinches a leaf and passes it around. Almost everyone likes this minty odor. This plant made a medicinal tea for Indians and pioneers "for whatever ailed them." However, we caution the group that, when ill, they had better see a doctor and get a regular prescription. Out on the open brushy slopes, there is coast sage or "old man" (*Artemesia californica*) and coffee berry or cascara (*Rhamnus californica*), whose parts yielded other medicines.

A real olfactory adventure is presented when the group gets under a California bay or laurel (*Umbellularia*). This famous California evergreen has pungent leaves that can be dried and used in flavoring foods. The naturalist invites his group to crush and sniff a leaf—just once. They may burst into tears or exhibit other symptoms of distress after a second or third sniff. Dangerous experiments for tenderfeet in the woods, you may ask? Maybe so, but we have yet to lose a sniffer or a taster on one of the hikes.

Campfire Girls meet poison oak—a warning in time.

In May or June after a season of good rainfall, there may be wild strawberries. But it is from late July and August onward that nature hikers really get the wild fruit treats. Wild blackberries, wild currants and gooseberries (*Ribes* species), blue elderberry (*Sambucus mexicana*) and California huckleberry (*Vaccinium ovalifolium*) are always ripe and free for the picking in some areas of the hills. They grow in the company of manzanitas, chamise brush (*Adenostoma fasciculatum*) and the rarer chinquapins (*Castanopsis chrysophylla* minor) with their chestnut-like seeds locked up in formidable burrs.

Avoiding trailside traps

Nature cannot be completely friendly and harmless. The "trailside traps" are waiting for the untutored and the unwary. It is up to the naturalist to introduce them before someone stumbles upon them.

Public Enemy Number One of the native flora is poison oak (*Rhus diversiloba*). And what an anomaly. It is surely the nemesis of the neophyte in the hills, but also valuable game and livestock forage and a good erosion control shrub.

Poison oak identifications along the trail never are finished because poison oak knows no set pattern or consistency of growth. First it creeps, then it climbs high on a pine or cypress, then perhaps presents itself in a massive thicket of six- to ten-foot high shrubs. Its three-grouped leaves may be an inch and a half long and deeply lobed or four or five inches long by three inches across and barely notched. All leaf buds open reddish in spring, become light to dark green, then turn red in early summer on sunny slopes or not until fall in heavy shade.

Every nature hiker should be well indoctrinated in how to know this infamous scourge. The experts say that only pure-blooded Indians were immune to it. But what happens after all our precautions and warnings? Next fall Mister Cub Packmaster or Missus Campfire Leader will help the boys or girls gather nice straight stems of the leafless poison oak for that cookout in the hills if they haven't learned their lesson well. The poison is right there in the stems too. What the handling doesn't accomplish, the smoke really does. What a cookout!

"Back on the trail, boys," the naturalist calls as some of the youngsters break lines and head down the creek bank to see what is in the shallow pools under the bank. And just in time. These eager nature explorers are about to push through a patch of tall, gray-leafed stems. They wouldn't soon forget the experience if they did. That's stinging nettle (*Urtica gracilis* var.). Stinging hairs on leaves and stems immediately cause painful welts on bare skin.

There are a few things not to be tasted too. Fortunately, Nature made them taste so poor, few humans will eat them. But some, like poison hemlock (*Conium maculatum*), grow so profusely everywhere along roadsides and in low ground that they must be identified and branded for what they are.

Poison hemlock, the cup Socrates drank on request, is an Old World weed with tall, succulent stems, carrot-like foliage, and whitish flower heads. Sweet fennel or licorice plant (*Foeniculum vulgare*) is also tall, succulent but nice to chew and may grow beside the hemlock. Attending a few guided nature walks will avert some mistakes.

Wildflowers to admire, but not to eat, greet the nature walkers from March to June. Buttercups, goldfields (*Baeria*), blue dicks and blue muilla (*Brodioea* sp.), wild hollyhock (*Sidalcea*), California poppies, silver bush lupine, sticky bush monkey flower (*Diplacus*), and a few wild sunflowers (*Helianthella* and *Wyethia*) color the route. With the drying grasses of June and July appear pink farewell-to-spring (*Clarkia*), gum plant (*Grindelia*), and a few yellow mariposas (*Calachortus luteus*).

Always an attention getter is the Indians' multiple-use plant, Indian soap root (*Chlorogalum pomeridianum*). Clumps of lily-like leaves growing on a sunny bank remind the naturalist to stop and demonstrate this amazing species. One plant must be pulled out of the loose soil and sacrificed for the demonstration, but it really won't be wasted. Some enthusiastic youngster will ask for it to take home and make the soap to his own satisfaction.

The audience learns how the California Indians used the stiff fibers surrounding the bulbous root for fish nets and brushes. If we carry the root down to the stream, we can quickly produce a soft lather from the white root. There are no fish in this creek or one or two might accidentally be "tranquilized" and float to the surface when the lather permeates the water. People are fascinated by this Indian trick and have to be warned that present fish and game laws frown on this operation. When they learn that the Indians could also leach out the bitter juices of soap root and use it for food, they are almost incredulous.

"Eye-spotters," "ear-spotters" and "trackers" are busy at the head of the naturalist's column. "I think I found mountain lion tracks!" a boy tracker shouts. Everyone rushes to surround the discoverer and his tracks in the mud. They are tracks of a big dog, we decide regretfully, but next time it might be a mountain lion's tracks. They have been seen along here.

What about the birds which must get some attention on a nature hike, even if we have stressed the botanical discoveries. We see some juncos and a couple of brown towhees to start with. Restless chickadees dangle on pine and cypress branches, while a nasal "yank yank" note helps locate a red-breasted nuthatch. Purple finches sing from tree tops, and the sharp-eyed Stellar jays scold loudly.

"That's the greatest by far," announced someone with an ear for music when a black-headed grosbeak sang from a bay tree. No one disputed this verdict.

Later on when "sickle-bill," the California thrasher, poured out his rich baritone notes, some ot the voice experts wanted to give him the top award. The measured, staccato trill of a little

171

wren-tit issuing from the same patch of chaparral was backstaged by the thrasher, but wren-tits are far more frequent and distinctive than any other bird song of this habitat.

"Hawk overhead!" some bird scout called out. Hawks are an attention getter, even for those who hardly notice the small birds. All necks crane as eyes go aloft, and it turned out to be not just one, but a pair of red-tails. They forage the year round over the canyons and very cleverly conceal their nest in spring.

This reminds the naturalist to tell the people about "Hawkeye," the redtail. This former pet living wild and free swooped in from the hills every day to catch meat tossed to him by his friends, the Rosenkranz family of San Leandro. This went on for several years until he swooped playfully on a strange pedestrian, and the "tac squad" shot Hawkeye on the street.

"Another hawk," someone interrupts. But this time it is a "T-V," the bird watcher's nickname for the turkey vulture. People ask how these big meat eaters which are unable to catch their own prey ever manage to find enough carrion in these hills to sustain them. We guess it is due to the miles per day they cover. Something dead is bound to turn up in such a range.

172

Getting back to the botany, a large branch of blue elderberry is jutting into the park fireroad. This is a chance to cut off a clean section of stem almost an inch and a half in diameter and scoop out the pith. When a notch is cut on top, we have an Indian flute. This was the Indians' "tree of music," as well as a source of delicious fruit.

There is a patch of horsetail on the lower side of the road. This straight stem with the whorls of rigid branchlets is a plant left over from past geologic eras when California was mostly a swamp where giant reptiles roamed. The stems can be pulled apart at the nodes with loud pops. Another name, "scouring rush," suggests to all that it can be used to clean camp pots and pans. A Swedish woman along told how her family made a dye of it.

And so another nature hike for the city folks came to an end. We didn't call it a "survival hike" but considering all the hazards they were exposed to without serious casualties, perhaps it was. Sometimes we forgot to mention the scorpions, centipedes, black widow spiders, or the rattlesnake very rarely found in these hills. However, somebody might later develop a little poison oak— like the kid who got off the trail. Accidents will happen.

Keeping the Peace
and Saving Some Pieces of Parks

Many kinds of "problem boys" haunt public places and are involved in frequent incidents in the principal parks. There are many classifications of these undesirable characters and of their misdemeanors or crimes. Most of them are left for the city police to handle unless they involve such obvious infractions as stealing or stoning birds, molesting animal exhibits, defacing trees or buildings, purse snatching, and the like. In such incidents, park personnel may attempt to arrest and detain the violator until the police can be called.

"Peeping Toms," "bushwhackers," and other curious characters who might be classified as "people watchers" with concealed motives are among the most annoying and at the same time the most amusing of park undesirables. The majority of them are quite harmless—just misguided or frustrated males who have departed slightly from the norm for masculine behavior.

Petting couples and female sunbathers naturally attract the largest gatherings of "peepers." Some "peepers" will take up positions in the open just a few yards away from the amorous couple or the sunbathers and stare like a circle of hungry wolves. Others will secrete themselves behind the nearest bush while still others will walk back and forth at frequent intervals, feasting the eye at

174

each passing. They are all extremely difficult types to discourage, and it is not easy to prove any malicious intent against them. Some, if arrested, would like to hire sharp lawyers and sue for false arrest.

One particularly obnoxious type of "people watcher" is the one who arms himself with binoculars. He may operate from his parked car or from a convenient bench not too far from his quarry. The victims of his scrutiny may remain quite unaware of it. But even if they do become aware and object to the nearest park employee or police officer, not much can be done about it except to check the miscreant's identification and learn if he has a police record. If he has, he'll usually be glad to move on after a warning. If he hasn't, he may claim he's merely watching the birds and literally thumb his nose at you.

"Peepers" go to greater lengths in the hill parks. One of the park rangers was startled while on a park patrol to see a man with a pair of binoculars perched high in a live oak. The ranger knew the source of his interest—a lovers' hideaway—but decided to teach the "peeper" a lesson. He quietly walked toward the tree— unseen by the "peeper"—and bellowed loudly. The guy dropped

his glasses and almost fell out of the tree. Then he took off. Rust-lings in the brush indicated his "victims" left almost as abruptly!

Among the senior citizens who daily frequent what we call the "Philosopher's Bench" at the Duck Feeding Area are several gentlemen who would like to wear the badges of honorary officers. These citizens do furnish a real service in warning or reporting many of the minor offenders who operate in this area, such as the pigeon snatchers, slingshot artists, and bicycle racers. When these same volunteer patrolmen branch out in the business of detecting and reporting more serious crimes, they sometimes become over-enthusiastic and bring down powerful forces of the law which may cause more inconvenience and embarrassment than did the sus-pected characters.

"Putting the finger" on suspected dope passers is one of the more exciting phases of volunteer sleuthing and one which gener-ally rings an alarm bell at police headquarters. Whether guilty or innocent, a suspect follows a pattern of spending considerable time in a public park and of daily meetings with other suspect persons.

A young man who had hung around Lakeside Park for some time gradually began to spend much idle time in the vicinity of the most popular children's play lot. This is not considered a desirable occupation of unattached men who have no children at play nearby. When this fellow was observed having an occasional rendezvous with other roving individuals in the same area, he soon became suspect as a "passer" as well as some variety of "Peep-ing Tom." On several occasions members of the naturalist staff joined the suspicious senior citizens in turning their bird binoculars on these rendezvous, but no positive incriminating evidence could be found.

Finally the weight of circumstantial evidence became too much for the volunteer sleuths, and the city police were called. Without expending much time in plain clothes "plants," the police took this principal suspect from his play lot post into a prowl car for questioning and investigation. It developed he was a state prison parolee and without any visible sources of support, though he had been seen mowing lawns and washing cars in the neighbor-hood. But try as they might, they couldn't get the goods on him and had to be satisfied with turning him loose with a warning.

The next day this released suspect appeared with an easel, canvas, and paint and set up his stand in the same play lot area!

176

Now he had an obvious reason for being there, one he thought the forces of the law wouldn't dare question. He was left undisturbed until he disappeared from the scene sometime later.

Speedboats versus the birds

The annual Fourth of July speedboat races on the lake inevitably result in some casualties among the bird population. On this particular Fourth, the birds were again caught unaware by the boats and, apparently, were reluctant to leave their accustomed waters with the first warning sounds of the warming-up period. By early afternoon, the crowd along the east shore witnessed an entire column of snow geese sailing stubbornly into the path of the careening boats. Desperate efforts were made by the pilots to avoid collision with the birds which suddenly, in alarm, split their dignified ranks. Boats swerved by within inches and somehow missed all but one of the flock. This goose received crippling injuries and flopped helplessly out of reach of would-be rescuers.

The speedboats went roaring on to their goals, but for hundreds of shocked observers the race was over when the bird was hit. One or more calls went to city hall and to the Oakland pound. Prowl cars and pound wagon were ordered to retrieve the wounded bird. They raced around and around the lake, but no crippled goose could be found. They called the Duck Feeding Area, but nobody had told us of the incident. In fact, we never did learn who rescued the crippled goose, or if it wound up at a veterinarian's office, in the morgue, or in a cookpot.

But the aftermath was yet to come. A sensitive and sympathetic lady residing on the lakeshore had observed this unfortunate incident. After first talking to city officials, she was referred to the Park Naturalist. Still in a state of indignation, she demanded to know why this accident was allowed to happen. "Before the races, why weren't the birds herded behind the safety of the log boom which encircles the Duck Islands?" she asked. Then we did recall that some years ago we had helped the Municipal Boathouse in just such a herding operation before the speedboat races. We quieted this overwrought bird lover by assuring her that on future Fourths we would drive the birds behind the boom before the start of the races. And heaven help us if we overlooked such an effort.

Another request from a sympathetic but quite unreasonable lover of the birds was that we construct some kind of shelter for the ducks during the rainy season. This, we tried to explain, was entirely needless, but we are still unsure this lady was convinced.

Still another disgruntled taxpayer resident of the lakeshore demanded to know how come the numerous mud hens were allowed to feed and leave manure on the lawns when her dog was prohibited from using them.

The duck dinner scandal

A chance meeting with a lawman, retired some years from police work, brought to light still another version of an unhappy episode in the recent history of the Lake Merritt Waterfowl Refuge. It happened in November, 1943, during the annual trapping and banding season for the Lake Merritt ducks.

What was the cause of it all? Perhaps it was the casual observation from a most respected citizen, Mr. Ehman, a protector of the wild ducks and long-time official government "cooperator" in this banding operation. He remarked that there were too many tame mallards to feed to the exclusion of some wild ducks at the Duck Feeding Area in Lakeside Park. The mallards constituted the permanent breeding colony of ducks on and around the lake, but they found life so pleasant there that they rarely, if ever, migrated like the pintails, widgeon, and others. Therefore, most serious bird watchers, students, and official bird banders frowned upon these mallards who refused to share the habits and the hazards of the real wild ducks.

One morning a couple of curious citizens lingering near the Duck Pond saw the regular caretaker "whistling in" the flock and baiting them into the big wire cage which served as a roundup trap. At first they thought this was a prelude to another duck banding session, and they stayed awhile to watch. But what followed puzzled and bothered them. They saw other park employees appear and separate a number of mallards from the wild ducks caught in the roundup. Then these mallards were quickly put into the back seat of a nearby municipal car.

Now mallards had frequently been removed or thinned out in past fall seasons and turned over to the County Hospital which had generally dispatched a truck to pick them up at the Duck Pond. Since these Lake Merritt mallards had been classified as "domestic ducks," this procedure had been accepted as legal and proper. But this new manner of shipment aroused the

178

suspicions of Mr. and Mrs. Plain Citizen, so they got into their car and followed.

Sure enough the carload of mallards was driven into a private driveway not too far from the park, and the ducks were unloaded there. That was enough for the citizen detectives. They immediately got in touch with the police, and the pots began to boil — both at the employee's home where the ducks were delivered and around city hall. And thus the famous "Lake Merritt Duck Dinner" rapidly took on headline status.

The local press boldly proclaimed, "U.S. PROBES DINNER OF LAKE MERRITT DUCKS" and "BANQUET OF CITY OFFICIALS UNDER INVESTIGATION," etc., etc. The Chief of

Police, the Park Directors, City Manager, the State Division of Fish and Game, the U.S. Fish and Wildlife Service, and other officials were in a huddle to determine whom and how to prosecute the case. Had the culprits merely violated a city ordinance, or State Fish and Game Code, or the Federal Migratory Bird regulations? And who gave the order to round up and transport the ducks to a private residence?

Police investigators soon found a park foreman who admitted ordering the roundup, but he immediately asserted that his orders came from city hall, and from an official of the department, no less. Then the investigators swooped down on the home of the

179

employee where the doomed ducks had been delivered. They even checked the garden for evidences of fresh burial of duck parts. It seemed they had also interviewed the women gardeners who had been hired with some misgivings "for the duration" of the war. Perhaps because these ladies hadn't been fully accepted into employees' circles or perhaps because their discretion wasn't trusted, they hadn't been invited. But they volunteered the information that there had been a duck dinner for certain selected employees and officials.

Digging up the gruesome clues

Meanwhile, the clue hunters came up with the heads, feet, and feathers of about a dozen mallards—all this unearthed in the back yard! And a number of those implicated had confessed to partaking of a duck dinner at the same address. In fact, some admitted to consuming one entire duck apiece, while others said they were served only half-ducks. At least twenty-eight employees and some officials had taken part in the feast. It was so delightful that the group present had voted to repeat it every month or so and to invite more guests.

The local sleuths and game officers went back to interview the officials implicated by these confessions from the rank and file. The official who wouldn't talk about it the previous day had now become more cooperative. Yes, he had attended the dinner, but they hadn't told him until after dinner where the entree had come from. And he certainly had never given any order to gather up Lake Merritt mallards for such a purpose. He and other officials had frequently given permission for surplus mallards to be sent to local hospitals or other public institutions, but that was all. So the investigators called in the park foreman, but he had since had a lapse of memory. He just couldn't remember who had issued the order to take them to that address where they were prepared for the ill-fated dinner.

This had become a most embarrassing and unsavory mess. It appeared that everyone concerned, except some indignant citizens, was most anxious to minimize the damage or, at least, to reduce this from a federal or a state case to a mere local law infraction.

A delegation of lawmen was dispatched reluctantly to the palatial home of E.W. Ehman, the prominent citizen and waterfowl authority. Although this man lay on his sickbed, they sought an important opinion from him concerning the status of the Lake Merritt mallards. He had been shocked to read about all this in the local press and to realize that it might have been prompted inadvertently by his expressed opinion that the mallards were too numerous at the Feeding Pond for the welfare of the true wild migrant ducks. But he now expressed the opinion that these mallards, hatched and reared for many generations right on Lake Merritt, were no longer "wild ducks" and therefore not entitled to protection of state or federal laws and regulations.

This expert's opinion was received by the culprits like the next best thing to a gubernatorial pardon. Visions of paying heavy fines or being sentenced to a penitentiary quickly passed away.

Now that the case was dumped back into the hands of the city officials, the city manager and the chief of police were quick to announce that possible punishment would be left to the Park Board. And the board hastily announced that it could only punish the employees involved for infractions of regulations, not as lawbreakers. Since a member of the board had partaken of the stolen fruit, interested citizens didn't look for any harsh punishment to be meted out.

An hour-long open hearing by the board, sitting in solemn judgment, centered mainly on that now-most-unhappy foreman who arranged the mallard roundup and delivery. His loss of memory concerning his "orders from higher up" continued to plague him, though he was warned that he would bear the full responsibility if he protected someone else. Finally in order for an absentee member of the board to have time to read the transcript, the board adjourned the hearing without decision.

So the forgetful foreman took the rap. He was banished from Lakeside Park to an outlying park, where no mallards would quack or strut to suggest another duck dinner. All parties concerned tried to forget and return to their peaceful daily routine. And the much-maligned mallards? Most of the survivors stayed right on at the lake and also carried on "business as usual," including the production of offspring in such surplus that more future roundups and removals would be called for. But no more for employee dinners!

Murder will out

If only those citizens with the sharp memories and sharp

tongues would forget the matter too. But the local sportsmen joined those still-indignant citizens who continued to carp about the duck dinner episode. It seems that the nationwide organization, Ducks Unlimited, had just launched a drive to collect the feathers of wild ducks and geese. The down of ten mallards would provide warmth and buoyancy for the suit of a downed flyer, the government had revealed. Now, what had been done with the plumage of those doomed Lake Merritt ducks? Why the culprits had just buried it!

Can the full story ever be told in such a celebrated case? A former park supervisor, Howard Cox and his wife Rose stopped off on a visit and were asked if they remembered this infamous incident.

"Do we remember it?" interrupted his wife. "Why for awhile we thought Howard and the other boys were going to Alcatraz."

She told how Howard had come home and said he wanted a bowl of potatoes for the duck dinner. She said, "You can't eat those ducks."

But Howard merely said, "Never mind, just give me the potatoes."

She went on, "Imagine my feeling a few days later when I saw the headlines before Howard came home from work. When he did come in, he looked like a hunted criminal."

Then they both told of the teasing they had to take during those trying times. They attended a rather large club meeting one evening and were a few minutes late in arriving. Upon entering the room, everyone started to quack! Little gifts began arriving in the mail—all of them ducks or associated with ducks. Even nature itself seemed to taunt them. One day a wild duck dropped from the sky and lay dead right in their front yard. Rose in her fright wrapped the duck and rushed it off to a neighbor's home lest the law find such a thing in their possession.

The late Jack Burroughs, an Oakland Tribune writer, penned some appropriate words in his column during those dreadful days of the duck dinner publicity.

> "Alas," the mallard murmured,
> "I am strictly out of luck.
> For a duck may be a mallard,
> But a mallard's not a duck.

> So farewell to old Lake Merritt,
> Refuge false for such as I.
> I am off for scenes more friendly;
> Lakeside Park, a fond goodbye."

Dog days in the park

Picture the scene if you don't have one in your city — a municipal downtown lake teeming with water birds, surrounded by acres of lawn where the birds want to feed, but invaded from dawn until dark by scores of restless, curious, yapping, or temporarily berserk canines. Then consider how much more critical the situation becomes when you have a dedicated, world-famous "waterfowl refuge" on this same lake where thousands of citizens and visitors expect to find the birds undisturbed, secure, and friendly.

We forgot to mention the blocks upon blocks of apartments and condominiums, ranging from modest proportions to a twenty-eight story high rise, that nearly encircle this particular scene at Lake Merritt. Among these prosperous city-dwellers, the canine count far outnumbers the child count.

What do you do with an exercise-starved dog when there is no back yard? Why, you walk him on the sidewalk or in the park. Better yet, if you're too busy to walk Rover, you turn him loose, counting on his good sense and his stomach to bring him back reasonably soon. What about your city's leash law? Well, if he's silly enough to get caught, we'll just bail him out at the Animal Shelter.

The result is the great year-round dog chase, featuring animal control men, park rangers, and the naturalist staff. Most of these people are really dog lovers themselves, but they are charged with protecting the birds and the other citizens who don't like to walk or sit in dog-doo.

What about that gang of kids from the inner ghetto who appear in the park accompanied by one to several nondescript frolicking canines? There's rarely even a leash among them, and when accosted, they'll admit ownership of one dog—or maybe none. Their mongrel friends aren't about to respond to calls, whistles, or stern commands. The kids seem to regard any uniformed man as a challenge to their liberty or civil rights. Secretly you

183

admire such good dog sense and you hate yourself for having to
bawl out the kids and order them to take their pets out of the park.

The "street people" present a stickier problem. They, too,
love their public parks and feel their dogs should know and love
them also. They are old enough to know about leash laws and to
read the signs excluding dogs from downtown parks. Some of
them even buy dog licenses and carry leashes or lengths of rope,
but it must injure their ids to have to restrain free canine spirits.

"Street people" are generally gentle folk and rarely argue or
threaten when accosted with their dogs. Sadly they regard their
brother of The Establishment who would destroy this lovely thing
of a man or woman and a dog in the park. We naturalists had no
citation books so we warned them that the next uniformed man
who came by would write them up to the tune of a monetary
fine. With this, they usually led the deprived dog away.

It is really amusing to watch the typical city-bred dog when
it spots a duck, goose, coot or gull on the lawn around the lake.
If the dog has any spirit, it will launch a noisy charge upon the
unfortunate bird. If judged by the speed, determination, and
sound, you would assume it was prepared to seize and tear its
victim to shreds. Of course, with this sort of approach the dog
rarely gets within reach of its objective, which promptly takes
wing for quieter spots. The frustrated hunter may even get as far
as the water's edge to bark a sad farewell to this lost quarry
which plays the game so unfairly.

Occasionally the brave pooch will overtake its victim—probably one of the heavyweight domestic ducks or geese so common
around any municipal duck pond. He may succeed in cornering it
against a fence or dense bush. What happens then?

"Grow-w-w! Snap-crunch!" The mighty hunter has a mouthful of feathers! The victim lashes out with its wings, and maybe
delivers a sharp jab or two in the canine chops. The dog backs up
quickly and surveys this creature with the unorthodox wrappings
and defense methods. By this time, his owner, the bird keeper,
and perhaps a chorus of aroused bird lovers are all yelling at one
bewildered dog which makes an on-the-spot decision to give up
this sport for something he can better understand.

A pair of geese or swans at the water's edge or on the lawns
with their brood of youngsters is another matter. The uninformed
dog that rushes them is in for deep trouble. The gander or the

cob (male swan) will meet the attacker half way. The dog will be lucky if he doesn't crawl off with a broken leg. If he jumps into deep water after the goose or swan family, he may be seized and drowned.

Are wild bushes dangerous to people?

If someone from city hall had come into Lakeside Park in the 1930's and announced to George Grimwood, the doughty park foreman, that the chief of police would hereafter supervise his tree and shrub pruning, Grimwood probably would have had that person escorted out of his office. Foreman Grimwood might even have treated everyone within hearing to some well-chosen British invective. Proposals to fell a tree or tear out a shrub bed for a new path or structure would have received a similar reception. And he would have been stoutly supported by most of his gardeners and nurserymen—a dedicated, green-thumbed crew of mostly southern European origin.

Across the bay in San Francisco, a hard-bitten Scot, Park Superintendent John McLaren, had defied city planners, engineers, and politicians who wanted to place buildings and new roads across *his* Golden Gate Park plantings. He was even known to work a crew all night throwing up new plant barricades against such threatened invasions.

Such dedicated defenders of park purity—and by this I mean the sanctity of naturalness, wildlife and botanic values—have gone to their rewards. But we need more park "career men" of their conviction and dedication today. They could join forces with the young "ecology action" groups. Trees and wildlife should rate "almost like people" in their thinking and let them take on the master planners who would carve up parks for freeways and public buildings. For a doomsday has come upon the public parks as they knew them and kept them. The Great American Crime Wave has brought a drastic purge to many of these once inviolate refuges from the sights, sounds, and smells of big cities. Let me draw a picture of those changes in a typical city park.

Oakland's Lakeside Park, when I first knew it in the days before World War Two, was a delightful wildness, surrounded by the city. There were wide open lawns and drier areas shaded by coast live oaks, holly oaks from southern Europe, turkey oaks from Asia Minor, and red and pin oaks from the Atlantic states,

Asiatic maples and a host of other stately trees brought from several countries and continents. There were also tennis courts, bowling greens and flower beds, lath-houses and greenhouses to attract citizens and visitors of various tastes and interests.

But the real retreats of wildness—a word I prefer here to "wilderness"—were the shrub beds, laid out by themselves or under trees. They consisted mainly of dense, evergreen shrubs. Lakeside's first landscape designer, Oscar Praeger, had selected from Australia, New Zealand, Mexico, subtropic America, and temperate Asia and the Mediterranean region species which he knew would flourish in this Bay Area climate.

Flowering *Veronicas* (now called *Hebes*), Tea-trees (*Leptospermum*), Brush-cherries (*Eugenia*), shrubby *Acacias,* and *Pittosporums* represented the Australian region; red-berry *Cotoneasters* and Fire-thorns (*Pyracantha*), *Raphiolepis*, *Abelias*, and evergreen *Viburnums* came from Japan and China; while southern Europe and Mediterranean climates furnished pomegranate, true myrtle, laurel-cherries (*Prunus* species), tamarisks, and a weird, spiny-branched butcher's broom (*Ruscus*). Neighboring Mexico had loaned California and Lakeside Park the little Mexican orange or *Choisya* and the showy Turks-cap or altar boy (*Malvaviscus*); while from the distant Andes had come a tribe of sticky-leaved *Excallonias* which reached fifteen feet or more in height.

This made up a rare assemblage of plants which could be grown out-of-doors only in such a hospitable climate along the California coast. San Francisco's greater Golden Gate Park had some years earlier been planted with similar exotics by park planners William H. Hall and John McLaren. Perhaps Oakland's Oscar Praeger had copied many of their achievements, except we know that he shunned *Eucalypti* and palms in his Lakeside scheme. Visiting botanists and horticulturists would all but swoon over this spectacle. I came to refer to it as a "United Nations of Plantings" and a "World Tour in Fifty Acres" as I conducted Oakland people and tourists through this informal arboretum. But these masses of shrubbery had many other purposes and uses.

Native birds loved these places and so did the bird lovers. Song sparrows and towhees (both the bold California brown and the timid rufous-sided or "chewink"), white-crowned sparrows and wren-tits hid their nests in dense bushes. Shy hermit thrushes, varied thrushes, hordes of migrant white-crowned and golden-crowned sparrows populated them in fall and winter. Cooper and sharp-shinned hawks swirled through in pursuit of these winter birds, or perched overhead and contemplated more daring attacks on the pigeons, wandering mud hens, or even a fox squirrel now and then.

Shrub hideouts for wild fugitives

To my knowledge only one bird ever took advantage of these shrubby retreats as ambushes from which to launch attacks on human passersby. That was a feisty ring-necked pheasant which had been released in the park in company with a hen or two. While his companions lived, "Cocky" didn't cause much trouble, but when he became the lone survivor, it must have embittered him. He began to attack various human females passing his haunts by flailing their ankles with his spurs!

We put up with Cocky for some months, in spite of a growing number of complaints. "Oh, that's just what a lot of barnyard roosters do," we would tell the irate victim. "Cocky really can't hurt you much—and he's the only wild pheasant we have left."

Some of the ladies were suggesting that we, the pheasant lovers, replace their torn hosiery. This was going too far. I reluctantly told the park staff that we couldn't protect Cocky any longer. He disappeared, and I preferred not to inquire of his fate.

Jack rabbits and ground squirrels escaped and took up residence in the shrubbery. These little fugitives were usually allowed to remain in their new habitats unless they moved into the horticultural show gardens for their meals. Then the cries, threats, and imprecations of the gardeners forced us to take action.

Did you ever try to trap, shoot, or otherwise get an educated, gun-shy rabbit out of a garden? If so, you probably dropped the phrase "dumb bunny" from your vocabulary. Morning after morning I joined the gardeners in a rabbit hunt in the gardens where they had dined copiously the night before. Unless we practically stepped on those jacks, they would remain frozen and secure. Unlike the fox squirrels, which could be baited with nuts into a live trap when they became pesty in the gardens, the bunnies stayed out.

Many human types took advantage of the shrubbery too. First, there were the children who found their little wildernesses here. They could hide from parents or playmates and then spring out upon the others with wild cries like Indians.

There were young lovers—couples who wished surroundings more natural than automobiles. And there were the older couples who loved those benches tucked into quiet, shrubby nooks away from the sights and sounds of nearby streets. Here they could talk, read, or doze away the hours.

Then there were the delinquents, but in those early years they were mostly winos and quite harmless to other park patrons. They needed most of all a quiet place to finish the bottle and sleep it off. And occasionally we would find a cache of Chinese lottery tickets which had been left in a bush by a wandering vendor. About the only incidents that required summoning the police to the park were those mornings when the "wagon" was needed to pick up a wino who couldn't get up and stagger back to town.

The 1950's and the '60's brought a burgeoning crime wave. First, the downtown streets became unsafe at night, then the city parks. Even the couples who sat in their cars along "lovers' lane" were sometimes accosted. And, worse yet, in broad daylight, hoodlums appeared out of the park shrubbery to snatch the purse or wallet from a passing citizen.

Personally, I would have preferred to see beefed-up park patrols employing motor-scooters or horses, and a plainclothes officer here and there. But, like so many modern cities, Oakland was committed to police patrols in prowl cars. Since these officers couldn't leave their cars for long to survey shrubby areas of parks, the bushes had to go—the possible ambushes, the wild retreats, and the birds.

What price security?

A great campaign of removal, thinning, and "lifting" hit Lakeside Park plantings, like other urban parks around the country. The man-on-the-beat must be able to see through and across from lawn to lawn and from street to street. What mattered the bushes, the botanists and nature buffs, or the birds? Parks must be made safe for people even at the cost of sacrificing some of the major purposes of these parks. Park naturalists and nature protectionist groups usually found their protests impotent in the face of panic-motivated drives. Fortunately most of Lakeside's grand old trees were spared as they couldn't so easily conceal miscreants.

School grounds and city playgrounds also suffered during this era of clearing and exposing all to view. Clumps of shrubbery, planted or natural, little weed patches, even the lower branches of trees which served as natural climbing forms—all have been swept away in these clean-out campaigns, regardless of the fact that they relieved the monotony of concrete and blacktop, or gave a few teachers opportunities to teach a little nature. Some degenerate, rapist, or other unwelcome type might hide in them!

The courses of brooks and creeks must also be cleared of all vegetation and concreted if possible. Muggers and degenerates might use them. Or, they backed up and overflowed into back yards during flood rains. And besides people filled them with litter. What if many children built dams, sailed homemade craft, or hunted snakes, minnows, and tadpoles in such places? They only cause trouble, said our engineers, police, and health authorities. Better cover them up!

So we have let the police and the people protectionists of many kinds have their way with our urban natural areas or spots of wildness. The hoodlums, thieves, and dope-pushers seem to be as numerous as ever. They get at the citizen without benefit of shrubbery ambushes, weed patches, or natural creeks. And this long campaign of clearing and denuding the urban landscape has got us into deep trouble of another sort.

A new concept of conservation has recently dawned upon this embattled country. Most Europeans knew it all the time, but we wouldn't listen. The concept is, simply: *preserve nature next door*—the urban environment. Educators, sociologists, conservationists, even some public officials and politicians are beginning to proclaim this truth.

How can you even hope to teach appreciation of nature—of ecology—to ghetto children if you have no examples left within reach? Many of these children will never see a national park or forest, a lake or beach, or at least not for some years. Colorful textbooks, television educationals and Disney true-life nature movies are fine, but still fall short of actual contacts—such as a tadpole or caterpillar in one's hand or watching a seed germinate and grow.

Now we have a growing host of teachers and professors demanding small natural areas or urban school grounds to introduce their new ecology teaching. City and suburban planners are beginning to call for the preservation of creek courses as "green belts" through new communities. A metropolitan park naturalist may even dare dream of the day when "spots of wildness" will again be permitted in all city parks for the sake of the children, the older folks, the lovers—and for the birds.

What about the muggers who might take advantage of such ambushes? Why not put on a nation-wide program of education in simple defense arts and tricks for respectable citizens of all ages? Let's have more critical attention by the citizenry to the sentences meted out to such law breakers when they are caught red-handed. Retired police officers and other trained older men frequent public parks and recreation centers and should be enlisted like "block wardens" to watch for and report suspicious persons in such places—even to assist in their detection and arrest when they commit assaults on park users.

And what of the "flower children" who sprawl across so many city parks and plazas? We condemn those who behave obscenely in public, bed down in shrub and flower beds, and scatter wine bottles and debris over the scenery. They must be punished and strictly controlled. But there is a large segment of these "nature children" who truly love and appreciate our parks. Why do not more authorities and conservationists try to enlist these people in protection of park values? The park they help you save from the developers might just happen to be your own.

Tar and Feathers

All was peace and tranquility on the northeast arm of Lake Merritt at the Waterfowl Refuge as the end of November drew near. The population of canvasbacks, scaup, ruddy, pintail, and widgeon ducks that frequents that protected body of water was far below the average of recent years, but that merely reflected a current duck decline up and down the western flyways during the fall of 1961. Those which survived the northern drought to reach Oakland were in fair shape and had resumed their usual feeding habits at the lake. The colony of resident Canada geese, after another successful nesting season, now numbered about fifty birds. The snow geese were gradually admitting the proud parents of two young broods back into their general society. Also five resident whistling swans, four European mute swans, and four Australian black swans graced the scene. Only the past Sunday had the Oakland Tribune carried a full page of pictures proudly showing the beauties of the lake and these birds.

191

Then disaster struck and all was changed. A frantic early morning call to my home was the first warning on this memorable Wednesday, November 29, 1961. A heavy oil flow had appeared along the shore and down into the duck feeding beach. Geese, swans, and smaller birds were already badly smeared. And it was pouring rain to make things even worse.

"Call the Street Maintenance Division to have a storm sewer check," I ordered. That is the usual procedure whenever oil appears on the lake.

A dismal picture greeted me at the duck feeding area. There were geese, ducks, and mud hens that were barely recognizable in their coats of heavy tar. They stood there vainly picking at their plumages. Offshore several more easily recognized swans, still whitish though badly discolored, floated out of reach while flocks of the resident mallards swam warily just beyond the affected area. The heavy sludge had accumulated and formed a pocket between the first island and shore. It did resemble tar more than oil

Snow geese become tar babies after Lake Merritt disaster.

and was so thick that floating debris was trapped and small objects thrown in experimentally actually rode on the crust.

At first some nearby garage was suspected of having dumped a quantity of crankcase drainings into a storm sewer. But it soon became evident that this material was continuing to pour in at the upper end of the lake and that prevailing winds were moving it on down toward the islands and feeding areas. Early in the afternoon one of the sewer inspectors brought us the word.

The offenders were a paving contractor and the State of California, Division of Highways. It was all an accident—or an act of God as they say in court. An emulsified asphalt preparation had been sprayed on the center shoulder of the link of new freeway being built across former park land just a block from the lake. The heavy rain prevented it from setting so it flowed down the bank and through the nearest sewer and into the lake. With forecasts of continued heavy rains, it appeared the oil would keep right on flowing.

It was obvious that a full-scale attack on this menace must be opened at once. Men and materials to cope with the oil flow were ordered for early the next morning, including the services of a power launch from the Recreation Department. But I knew from previous minor disasters of a similar nature that our municipal forces were not well organized to handle such oil flows on the lake. I called the Coast Guard as I remembered once before getting helpful advice from them. A fellow at the district office referred me to the U.S. Army Engineers who were supposed to have discovered a workable oil treatment substance.

This call struck pay dirt. We were given the name of a San Francisco chemical company that had recently demonstrated and sold a new liquid oil dissipator to the Army Engineers, Navy Department, and the Department of Fish and Game. When we called the company's chemist, he insisted on coming over in person to demonstrate his magic formula. This he did and most convincingly, working from both the bank and from a fragile rowboat in that torrential downpour. Then he arranged for us to pick up several gallons the next day. Not a cent for services or materials would they accept.

Help Unlimited

Supervising the efforts to check the oil flow, to build

emergency log and wire-rope-burlap booms to contain it, to start a roundup of tarred birds and provide reasonably clean outdoor pens to hold the birds were enough to keep the naturalists and bird keepers busy. In addition there were the reporters and cameramen to meet and to serve, and there was a rising wave of telephone calls from editors, the curious, and willing volunteers.

On the weekend, a letup in the rainstorm led us to decide to postpone actual pickup of the remaining oiled pockets until Monday. But there were still innumerable birds to pick up and clean, and we had in good faith told the press that more manpower and boats were needed for this. So now the telephone really went wild. Even the city hall operators said they could hardly cope with the calls.

Did we get our manpower and boats? Well, I must refrain from using the adjectives to describe the response. The offers of small boats didn't come so fast but that we could accept those we needed and hold off on the others. But the manpower—and especially the "boypower." We tried to dispatch only the experienced boys to go out in the skiffs to round up oily birds and to send men to supervise them. Even here we had to take chances, and at least two boys fell overboard into shallow water and had to be rushed home for drying and cleaning.

The "bird dry cleaning service" had been set up under a spacious workshed in the Lakeside Nursery area. At first only kerosene was used on rags as plumage swabs. Then a service station grease-absorbent powder made from rice hulls was tried and found quite effective. Later a local science teacher, who had once essayed manufacture of cleaning compounds, brought one of these powders. It was based on Fuller's earth as a principal ingredient and worked so well that we immediately bought a hundred pounds from him.

A former city nurse, a scoutmaster, a retired gardener, and several citizens who frequent the park to feed and admire the birds, quickly formed the bird-cleaning crew. Many others came to help on this operation or crowded around to watch the laundering. But these original workers stayed with the job, battled with the reluctant geese, swans, ducks, and mud hens, and tried to answer endless questions through clouds of dust and feathers. A steady stream of birds was carried back and forth between the lake, the holding pens, and this first aid bird laundry.

194

Some of these devoted bird rescuers had already asked to take birds home for further cleaning and recuperation and were given permission to do so. Then on Saturday night, some vandals broke into one of the holding pens and left a score of duck heads behind, taking even these poor oiled carcasses for a free meal or for pure meanness. The next day we decided to take most of the swans and some of the geese to a cooperative bird farm in Castro Valley for security. Volunteers who could still accomodate birds in basements or garages took more home.

Sunday brought new ranks of would-be bird rescuers. Not all these recruits could be accepted and supervised, which left not a few disappointed and disgruntled. Those who continued the bird roundups on lawns and around the duck islands could no longer catch the now-frightened birds and were causing more consternation and damage to the birds' feeding and resting pattern than the results justified. The big chase was finally stopped, but it was plain to see that this was not well received by some, and a few did protest to my superiors.

The public continued to come down in droves to see the "tar-and-feather birds" as the press labeled it. Many regular visitors were incredulous at finding the familiar feeding area almost bare of birds. Such total desertion of this all-important dining area was unknown to the public.

Within a few days all the asphalt slick had been removed from the Refuge end of the lake. Most of the geese and tamer ducks that required cleaning had been rescued and some of the good folk who had taken some home were beginning to return with carloads of restless fowl. There were touching scenes of reunion as separated domestic and wild geese found old friends and relatives. Eager volunteers and curious citizens stopped phoning and only one thoroughly dedicated couple continued to carry on some cleaning operations. Gradually the naturalists and other employees recovered from the roughest ordeal in many years of running this city bird refuge.

Waiting for the big spills

But news items of tanker collisions and oil spills around the world began to haunt me as the feeling grew that the coast, yes, even San Francisco Bay would soon witness an oil disaster that would make the Lake Merritt affair look like a mere incident. The Torrey Canyon tanker disaster of March, 1967, in the British Channel did cost the lives of thousands of sea birds despite heroic rescue efforts by British and French bird lovers.

Bird rescuers and launderers restored these victims to flight.

The California coast got its first catastrophic oil bath on February 1, 1969, when that gooey monster escaped from an off-shore well in the Santa Barbara Channel and rushed upon the nearby beaches. Diving ducks, grebes, loons, cormorants and other water birds were trapped and befouled. A colossal rescue operation was set up. Scores of Bay Area bird lovers, including several Audubon associates and a prominent veterinarian, rushed down there to assist. I'd have liked to join them, but my conviction grew that we would again have oil on our hands soon enough.

It happened to San Francisco Bay on a very foggy morning in January 1971. Two Standard Oil tankers collided just within the Golden Gate. As they locked together, thousands of gallons of Bunker C type oil spilled into the bay. Total estimates of the spill ran up to three quarters of a million gallons.

The inbound and outbound tankers should never have been permitted together in this treacherous narrow passage, it was admitted by almost everyone concerned a few weeks later during the hearing on the disaster.

"There is a large oil slick spreading on San Francisco Bay!" This stomach-gripping, chilling bulletin hit thousands of bay region people who listened to the news at breakfast that morning. It shook up the most those listeners who had previous tastes of oil disasters.

"Oh, God, the canvasbacks," was my first thought. San Pablo Bay, the northern portion of San Francisco Bay, is normally the principal winter resort for this famous diving duck on the Pacific Flyway. Midwinter counts have ranged as high as 90,000 for this species. Would the black ooze from a wrecked oil tanker wipe out most of this flyway population? There were also thousands of scaup and scoter ducks and grebes to worry about.

But the tides and the tremendous currents of San Francisco Bay were to prevent this particular catastrophe. Even before they carefully separated the locked leviathans, an ebbing tide was carrying a major portion of the black slick out through the Golden Gate. Bays, beaches, and sea-cliffs for many miles north and south of the "Gate" received the impact of the invader. The oil that remained within the bay affected several marinas and small beaches, plus a few thousand scoter ducks and grebes.

This time Standard Oil moved in immediately with a vast fleet of ships, barges, oil-skimmers, trucks, and earth-movers to take on the monster they had loosed. One huge skimmer-rig was

flown overnight in sections from the Gulf Coast, welded together
at their Richmond shops, and put to work offshore the next day.
Hundreds of regualr employees and "hard-hats" hired on the spot
spred hay and removed oiled-hay from the beaches. Hundreds
of volunteers—high school and college students, hippies, entire
families—joined them.

"Audubonites and Ecology followers to the rescue," might
have made other headlines because those two volunteer organizations jumped in feet first and up to their ears, almost literally,
in the bird rescues and cleaning operations.

The refuge outpost of the National Audubon Society on
Richardson Bay, inside and just a few miles north of the Golden
Gate, was immediately offered assistance from the U.S. Sixth
Army Presidio Headquarters, the Navy, and the Marine Corps.
Boats operated by the Department of Fish and Game, Sea Scouts,
the oil company, and volunteer skippers were picking up befouled
birds, which were then rushed to Richardson Bay, and to other
Marin County, San Francisco, and East Bay treatment centers.
Men, women, and children poured into these bird first-aid depots.
Many carried in the bird victims tenderly wrapped in cloths or
sacking. Others brought armsfull of paper, rags, and other cleaning materials.

Coordinating Operation Rescue

The Ecology Center of Berkeley, a fast-growing organization
that started with a few University of California students, professors, and sponsors, undertook the colossal task of coordinating all
bird rescue efforts on their side of San Francisco Bay. They set
up a bird cleaning and recovery center in an old warehouse in
Richmond. This soon became the biggest and most successful of
all such operations around the bay.

Who bought the frozen fish, the special pellet mixtures
for the diving ducks, the sandwiches and drinks for the hungry
volunteers working three shifts around the clock? And the
gallons of mineral oils, vast quantities of corn meal and flour
used to clean and dry the birds, tons of rags and newspapers?
All were cheerfully donated by hundreds of households, together
with many other assorted supplies given by neighborhood gro-
cers and druggists. Standard Oil provided some materials and
manpower.

A Battle of the Booms was meanwhile being fought at the mouth of Bolinas Bay, some twelve miles north of the Golden Gate. Students and teachers of the College of Marin, staffers of the Point Reyes Bird Observatory, and local residents worked alongside oil company hard-hats to block the entrance of Bolinas Bay to the tide-borne slick. They were desperately defending the feeding flats and waters of the famed blue herons and egrets of Audubon Canyon Ranch. In a few weeks these spectacular fishermen would gather to nest in the towering redwoods facing this bay. An oil-polluted bay bottom might reduce their fish and invertebrate harvest to the point where their young would starve and then this showplace rookery would disintegrate. (Already, pesticides in their food chain were rapidly reducing their nesting success and percentage of young reared.)

Swarms of volunteers, including many colorful hippie types, public agency and oil company people, the curious, and the press, at times blocked solidly the one main street of the little town of Bolinas. The town policemen tried bravely to cope with this extraordinary invasion. While I watched, two big

After the Golden Gate spill: beach cleaners at Agate Beach.

199

rigs loaded with portable latrines arrived on the scene and really stopped traffic.

"This must be something like a World War Two beachhead on the English Channel," I remarked to my companion photographer, "only with civilians and no shooting."

The battle against the oil at Bolinas Bay was won within a few days. Over on Point Reyes National Seashore, the invasion threat to Drake's Bay, Limantour Estuary with its wintering waterfowl, and Drake's Estuary with its precious oyster beds had passed. Park Service crews, oil skimmer rigs, the Johnson Oyster Company people, bird lovers, and volunteers had worked night and day out on this frigid, windy peninsula.

Cleanup of the more remote beaches and coves would require many weeks. The Army had bulldozed a berm across the entrance to Rodeo Lagoon, just several miles north of the Gate. Restoration of the delicately balanced tidepool life of Duxbury Reef, just over the point from Bolinas, might require months. The processes of recovery would furnish an invaluable outdoor laboratory for students.

The crusading Sierra Club, with its home base almost within view of the tanker collision, launched a virulent attack on the oil company and on the system which had set the stage for such a disaster. The Coast Guard speedily ordered public hearings on the incident. New headlines, television and radio broadcasters kept it spread before the public. Editorial writers and commentators proclaimed that something must be done about these tankers—there must be a control over their channel and harbor movements at least as effective as that exercised over airport traffic. Lawsuits totalling astronomical sums were entered or proposed against Standard Oil.

But the tar-and-feather victims—the water birds—continued to draw the most attention and sympathy! Their plight appealed far more to the public than reports on hearings and demands for stringent regulations. Graphic, heart-rending pictures of the birds and their devoted human nurses were hungrily seized by city editors and spread across the dailies. Closeups of coeds and long-haired boys covered with bunker oil acquired in their rescue efforts lent both comic and pathetic touches to these pictorials.

Cleaning the birds

Community bird reception and cleaning stations were set up

in cities on both sides of the bay. They were manned by house-
wives, street people, children . . . anyone who would lend a hand.
Most of these bird rescuers had never before held a wild water
bird in the hand. I suspect that more bird lovers than birds were
saved. Excessive handling is a very traumatic experience for a wild
bird and the delicate necks of grebes and loons can be permanent-
ly damaged if carelessly handled.

At Richmond a great corps of volunteers, supervised by a
few biologists and veterinarians, gradually worked out a cleaning
and recovery operation that should have won acclaim from the
Red Cross or Armed Forces human disaster experts. They bathed
the victims in mineral oils and light petrolatum supplied by
Standard Oil. After cleaning and drying, the victims were placed
in the "intensive care" section where visitors were admonished to
speak in whispers. Workers in white coats hovered over their patients.

Next, the birds were moved into separate wire cages carefully
covered with sacks or rags; later they went into open pens with
their own kind, still bedded on soft materials. Heat lamps of every
known make maintained a warm room temperature. Finally, some
genius brought in sea-and-surf recordings to further enhance this
artificial environment for the water birds. The music probably
did more for the nursing staff! But I was startled to hear two
common loons giving their mating song—something I'd never
heard before in their winter range along the coast, bays and
estuaries.

Live fish—vast numbers of tiny mosquito fish—served in
shallow pans may have accounted for the higher survival rate of
grebes and loons at the Richmond "hospital." On each pen and
cage, there was a medical record tag with careful entries of feedings and of terramycin dosages. The vitamin B additive, so essential
to diet when only frozen fish is fed, became unnecessary with
the live fish.

Over a hundred grebes, two hundred and fifty scoters, nine
murres, and eight loons were surviving almost a month after arrival
at Richmond. That represented a record rarely matched in the
growing history of tar-and-feather disasters. Still, many weeks,
even months, of confinement and care faced most of these birds.
Ultimately they would require "hardening off" in outdoor quarters.

A new recovery center was finally found up on a north bay
marsh refuge belonging to the Nature Conservancy. After some
weeks of indecision, threats of cutting off funds, and protests

from bird lovers, Standard Oil agreed to finance the recovery operation until September 1, 1971.

Meanwhile, the East Bay veterinarian who brought back Santa Barbara oiled bird victims for experimental treatment, Dr. James Naviaux, had again loaded the hospital at his Wildlife Health Foundation with victims of the bay spill. Carefully chosen volunteers labored over his patients while the Doctor and Mrs. Naviaux supervised and took careful notes on medications, feeding, and the birds' reactions. The oil company eventually gave a substantial sum toward the costs of Dr. Naviaux's operations.

Among the experts who flew to the Bay Area to give advice and physical assistance immediately after the oil disaster was the young scientist, Phillip B. Stanton, who had organized the "Wildlife Rehabilitation Center" at Upton, Massachusetts, financed by the American Petroleum Institute. After experiments with oil-soaked water birds from the Atlantic Coast to Santa Barbara, Stanton had adopted the new detergent, Polycomplex A-11. He believes the quick cleaning made possible by this method is far better for the victims than the twenty to forty minutes required by the mineral oil bathing process. He refused to force feed but worked out an intricate process of feeding and exercise over long periods for his patients. His success with species like scoters and loons has been phenomenal, according to an article in the Massachusetts Audubon Society Bulletin of October 1970.

What to do next time?

Accusations against the oil company and various public agencies were being flung back and forth long after the crisis of oiled birds and beaches had subsided. Some officials of the Department of Fish and Game and biologists insisted it would have been kinder to the oiled birds to have destroyed them all immediately. The British government was reported to have adopted such an official policy after a series of costly and frustrating oiled bird rescues.

How can such enormous wastes of human energy and emotions, helpless birds, and time and space in communications media be avoided in future oil spill disasters? I would urge that panels of biologists, state departments of fish and game or conservation, U.S. Bureau of Sports Fisheries and Wildlife, and other professionals be established to examine all available facts and determine the most efficient methods of cleaning and recovery of oiled water birds. Let us have a plan something like the American Red Cross Disaster

202

Services for these oil spill victims. And why shouldn't the oil drillers and tanker operators or their insurers establish an adequate contingency fund to handle the rescue and rehabilitation costs unless such expensive recovery operations were to be abandoned as an official policy? In such a case the contingency fund might be used to buy and restore shore and marsh habitat to counter-balance the bird losses, as such birds cannot practically be replaced by man-controlled propagation like chickens, turkeys, quail, or pheasant.

Now suppose you should happen upon a badly oiled water bird while walking along your favorite beach. It could be Los Angeles or Long Island, Lake Erie or the Mississippi—almost anywhere on public waters these days.

If you are the realistic, completely scientific type, you will quickly twist its neck or by some other method put it out of its misery. This will save the victim—and you and your family and friends—days and weeks of discomfort and trauma.

But if you must accept the role of rescuer and nurse, here are a few steps to follow. Wrap your patient immediately in a gunny sack, old clothing, or newspapers and get it to a fairly warm place as soon as possible. Cover the eyes or even the entire head loosely before you begin the cleaning process. If oil has penetrated into the under-plumage, a bath will be required. Use one of the new biodegradable detergents like the industrial Amberlux for a fast job; mineral oils and sulphonated castor oil may be used, but these take longer. Follow the bath with a lukewarm water rinsing, perhaps repeated. Corn meal and flour, rice hulls, talcum, or just rough rags will accomplish the rough drying off. Completion of the drying process may require heat lamps to 90° F installed over one part of the birds' pens. Never use infra-red lamps because of possible damage to the eyes.

Your recovery quarters should be kept around 60° F in winter and as close as possible to 70° F in summer, advises Mr. Phillip Stanton. Pens must have soft flooring materials to prevent breast and foot sores, but avoid hay or straw litter which may carry infection. Drinking water should be available during the first two weeks. After that the birds may have shallow bath pens or ramped swimming pools not over 18 inches deep. And watch them—they might even drown!

Now for the nitty-gritty of feeding. Fish-eaters like grebes, loons, gulls, terns, murres, and cormorants, must have fish, shellfish, or similar fare. If you cannot get small live fish, be sure to completely thaw the frozen kinds, and you may include small portions of moist, meaty dog food and drops of Vitamin B.

Most of the diving ducks will thrive on trout chow, pellet form dog meal, and game bird chows. Grit and oyster shell must be added if you keep the birds very long. Mallards, pintails, widgeons, and other dabbling ducks should get game bird chow, grains, and chopped greens.

Watch for dry, cracked legs and feet and treat them with vaseline or mild ointments. Terramycin is an excellent dosage for lack of apetite and other symptoms of decline, but you should get the proper dosage from your veterinarian or poultry supply dealer.

Good luck, my bird nurse friends. Remember, you may have your patients for months until they moult and regain their normal plumage. Meanwhile, you better notify the nearest game warden or wildlife protection agent of what you are doing, since the patient in your possession is a federally protected bird species. Some states have laws or regulations to cover just such humanitarian rescues. If it is a wholesale tar-and-feathers disaster, the authorities should designate some S.P.C.A., zoo, Audubon center, or a college conservation department to take the victims off your hands.

Supertankers bring superspills. The supertanker Metula that cracked up in the Strait of Magellan in August, 1974, carried 196,000 tons of oil. We dread to see these unwieldly behemoths carrying Alaska oil down the Pacific coast. Oiled birds and marine mammals make headlines, but what about the more lasting effects on fisheries, shellfish, and tidepool life? Must coastal wildlife and resources drown in oil before satisfactory substitutes are found or oil runs out?

Under pressure of aroused public opinion, lawsuits, and threats of legislative action, our major oil companies have formed or sponsored financially some eighty-nine organizations equipped to handle various types of oil spills. For example, an organization known as "Clean Bay" and supported by ten oil companies is on call night and day to rush out a task force to cope with any spill along the Northern California coast or in the San Francisco Bay Region. We watched their efficient handling of a rather small oil flow into Lake Merritt. Somebody suspected a nearby service station as the source, called company offices, and presto—Clean Bay arrived with the dispatch of a fire department and went to work. It developed later that that particular oil came down the creek from an undetermined source, but the oil company picked up the tab in the interest of their public image!

Out of the months of round-the-clock toil, sweat, and teamwork which followed the Great Oil Spill of San Francisco and these treatment stations, a new group was formed calling themselves the International Bird Rescue Research Center. This Rescue Center took over a floor of another warehouse belonging to the Berkeley S.P.C.A. Here David Smith and Alice Burkner, with a faithful crew of volunteers, advised by one of that breed of men we've dubbed "ecology vets," Dr. James Harriss of Oakland, carried on waterfowl rescues and rehabilitation with the crudest of equipment and facilities. Classes were established to train new volunteers.

Another eviction confronted these indomitable workers when their quarters were promised to a company that could afford to pay rent. Just in the nick of time the city of Berkeley agreed to lend them the use of a small building on the shores of the Berkeley Aquatic Park. The International Bird Rescue Research Center enlisted a number of dues-paying members and supporters to meet expenses. An exercise yard, family size portable swimming pool and guard dogs were installed. Small-scale oil spills in the bay and along the coast brought in scores of patients. The U.S. Coast Guard and other federal and state authorities began to order payments from offending ships and oil companies to defray the manpower costs at the Center. David Smith and Alice Burkner became known as waterfowl rehabilitation authorities and are now invited to fly to distant disaster sites to supervise or advise on rescues.

Saving ducks from botulism

Western Duck Sickness, known to professionals as Botulism C, hit the Lake Merritt ducks early in September 1971. A hot spell combined with inadequate circulation over shallow areas of the lake set the stage. Some gull that had fed on carcasses at a stricken sewage plant a few miles away may have brought the lethal infection, but this type of botulism, like Salmonella, lies dormant in most bodies of fresh or brackish water awaiting a signal. Thousands of wild ducks had already died that summer from the interior valleys of California to the Bear River marshes of Utah.

That Labor Day weekend the naturalist staff and volunteer youths had been carrying in the pitiful, limp mallard victims from shallow waters around the lake and from pools on the Duck Islands. Remembering a similar experience of some years before, I used a large rubber enema syringe to flush out orally quite a few living victims and establish them in makeshift hospital pens. Then the local press heard about it.

Like a band of ministering angels, appeared the "Ecology Vet," a charming and efficient student trainee, and several of the young people from the International Bird Rescue Research Center. They took charge like veterans. For almost two weeks they treated our staff, the media, and hundreds of passing citizens to a demonstration of how to handle a bird medical disaster. They even brought sleeping bags and slept beside their charges outside the Science Center. (City regulations prevented us from turning over the building to them after hours.)

We helped with the daily boat patrols and searches of the islands where the casualties were picked up. As the victims were brought ashore, the hospital facilities expanded. Converted cartons, cut out and set on end, formed the individual "wards" for the sick mallards. A weird array of plastic dish pans, baking pans, mini sinks, and baby baths were lined out in front of the wards. Bales of straw and newspapers for bedding loomed nearby.

The first aid station operated in GI fashion. Every patient got the oral enema of a 5% epsom salts solution in fresh water, to be repeated with straight water flushing two hours later, and again at lengthened intervals while in "intensive care." A drop in each eye, and the victim was off to its little ward to recuperate. This was certainly a far more simple operation than oil removal.

The results were gratifying. Out of three hundred and fifty mallards, resident geese, and domestic ducks stricken, the rescue team saved at least two hundred. As the patients reached the ambulatory stage, they were whisked off to a "halfway house" for complete recovery, then turned loose on cleaner waters in the north bay. Meanwhile, city authorities had cooperated by revving up the pumps that changed the lake water and by sending fire department pumps to improve water circulation by sucking in shallow water and spraying it out in gigantic streams.

The impact of the bird rescuers on the people who passed, paused, and gazed in wonderment was something else. Most of these young workers were shabbily dressed, often barefoot, and the boys wore long hair and were unshaven. But, here for God and all the world to see, they were ministering to helpless creatures, restoring them to life. They were unpaid and obviously existing on hamburgers and soda pop.

Prosperous, solid citizens from the swank apartments nearby learned that long hair, ragged breeches, and bare feet do not necessarily mean a wasted life and a burden to society. A few opened their hearts and their pocketbooks. Bags of homemade sandwiches were contributed, and at least one lady from the nearest highrise complex insisted that a rescue team have lunch with her one day.

When the Rescue Center workers finally dismantled their duck hospital, cleaned up the heaps of boxes, papers and straw, and departed, they had won our hearts as well as the battle against botulism C, even if we had mopped up their muddy footprints from back door to office, ran their telephone messages, and argued sternly with them about the merits and philosophy of lavishing tender care on afflicted gulls which would be devouring ducklings when spring came.

Another major breakthrough promising better care for wild birds and animals which become injured, sick, or oiled was the establishment of a National Wildlife Health Foundation. Dr. James L. Naviaux, of Pleasant Hill, and other veterinarians formed this organization to encourage their brother practitioners across the nation to treat wild animals. Under this plan, three hundred veterinarians in the United States and Canada participate in one of three categories: give all-out treatment to wild animals, offer restricted time or advice, or give advice only in disaster situations. None of them would be obliged to give free service to people's wild pets.

Unless you are fortunate in living near such a public-spirited vet or rescue center, you may find yourself alone with an injured, sick, or oiled water bird to treat. We hope the information in this chapter will help you in such an event. Remember to notify the nearest game warden or wildlife protection agent of what you are doing, since your patient will probably represent a protected species.

Naturalists in the Making

*H*ow would you tame a group
of teenage (or younger) boys and girls who are gung-ho to handle,
feed, and show off wild animals—the larger and more dangerous
the better? Can they be enlisted as staff helpers and taught safe
and sane methods of handling wild creatures before serious damage
is inflicted on themselves or visitors? Wouldn't staff be better off
just carrying on without these eager beavers? These days city hall,
city attorneys, counsels for the victims or their families—and
juries too—are ready and willing to heap blame and punishment
on the naturalist or teacher who allows a daring enthusiastic helper
to get hurt on the premises.

Perhaps we just didn't consider these liabilities—or uncon-
sciously decided to live dangerously—when we began accepting
promising boys and girls in the early years of the naturalist program

208

of the Oakland Park Department. I'll admit that we gambled in a few cases, and once in a while lost one, but the overall benefits to all concerned were incalculable. In the process of helping these kids overcome frustrations and fulfill their aspirations, we found that our lives and many of those who watched, talked, or listened to these junior aides were enriched. I often suspected that an admiring audience was as fascinated by the manner and style used by John, Paul or Nancy to introduce a skunk, possum, or snake as they were by the animal itself. People expect their salaried naturalists to be pros and take it for granted. When youngsters of ten or twelve begin performing like pros, everybody takes notice!

These young naturalists first performed routine tasks such as handfeeding of lizards which requires patience and deft fingers, feeding orphan birds and mammals, helping sort pigeons and tame ducks after a mass trapping to purge the colony, and preparing menus for the caged birds and mammals. There were also frequent duties assisting the naturalists with collections and exhibits within the Natural Science Center.

The most distinguished volunteer service of all was the "animal talk and demonstration" both at the Center and at summer day camps. This "animal talk" included introduction of small pets-of-the-season from black widow spiders to ducklings, baby hawks, owls, raccoons, and possums, and required boys or girls who could present a few facts as well as the animals in order to answer questions and protect the animal while allowing visitors to touch it. This was really quite a big order for a young volunteer.

Allowing junior volunteers to give pet shows serves a dual purpose: partly to relieve the naturalists on busy days and partly to develop the youngster as a guide, public speaker, and junior public relations person. Interest and concern for humans is also part of a naturalist's job so the talents and versatility of each aide was used to provide an outlet for self-expression and development.

Have you ever thought of using a lizard or snake to eliminate stuttering? No, this isn't a type of folk therapy. Take the case of Paul who came to the Center with a mild stutter. Snakes and lizards were his obsession. They were unwelcome at Paul's home, but at the Center, he could handle them, feed them, nurse the sick, coax the non-feeders, and go out collecting others. What was most important, he could show them and tell others all he knew about them. He gave "snake talks" at day camps and for impromptu audiences at the Center. Because Paul could speak with self-assurance on the things he knew well, he spoke each day with less stuttering—a satisfying reward to hear him improve his speech. Today Paul is an articulate teacher and lecturer with no trace of any speech impediment.

John and Dave arrived as a brother team, and, like most of the other junior aides, often carried the ball in lowly chores like cage cleaning and food preparation, when the regular staff was hard pressed. John, the older, also took home some live bats to feed, which wound up flying in and out his bedroom windows. Skip was drawn to us by his attraction to reptiles, and performed brilliantly in presenting (and winning friends for) his favorites. "Big Frank," a cheerful twelve-year-old, came to us from a Boy Scout family, worked cheerfully at the most humble tasks and, we liked to think, gained knowledge and purpose which led to that coveted Eagle Scout rank.

We broke the rule of a minimum starting age of twelve when we took on Jim, Dave, and Bob who clamored for chances to prove themselves. In fact, we might have been charged with nepotism; they were all related to the staff. I resisted, reconsidered, weakened, and finally accepted them for light duty—Jim and Dave at age eight, Bob somewhat older. The exceptions to the rule were justified. All three boys worked like Trojans for years until high school and then college brought them paying part-time jobs elsewhere. Jim is now a full-fledged park naturalist; Dave anticipates a career in natural science; and Bob has established himself in a municipal electrical department.

Alex—shy, studious, and fastidious—scion of a Russian refugee immigrant—was delicately introduced because he needed a "father image" as well as an opportunity to use his talents. Within weeks he was giving impromptu lectures to visitors, caring for the "Back Room Baby Zoo" even swabbing cages when the animal-keeper was unavailable. Alex, unlike many boys, liked flowers and welcomed the opportunity to learn more about wildflowers by helping with the continuing floral display rack. Later when invited to his beautiful home, he showed his collection of wildlife postage stamps, displayed and labelled with exacting accuracy and organization. Serving as a volunteer converted this shy boy into one who could confidently participate in any group.

210

"Little Paul" came to us in an extraordinary way. At age eleven he became so enthusiastic about Oakland's parks, the lake waterfowl, and the naturalist program that he wrote to the mayor requesting a "junior seat" on the Park and Recreation Advisory Commission. He was inspired by reading about a young woman student who had won such a place in a neighboring city.

His honor the mayor considered this unusual request, inquired further into Paul's interests and hobbies, then suggested that the lad become a Science-Center junior aide. The volunteer force was already up to full strength, but another happy exception was made. Paul turned out to be an expert on local reptiles which he loved to introduce and explain to enraptured listeners, as well as clean and feed them. There is no doubt that some day Paul could be a knowledgeable asset to some Park and Recreation Commission.

Jim, the young biology student

"Biologist Jim Carlton" came as a snooper of Lake Merritt shores and waters. Even at this junior high stage we spotted him as a future scientist. He worked alone and unobtrusively, but would usually come into the Center with his dip nets, jars, and magnifying glass to show us his finds. Before long Jim was providing complete lists of the invertebrate animals of the lake and its shoreline, teaching the occasional boy or girl aide who showed interest in such lowly animals, and giving Sunday slide presentations to mixed audiences at the Science Center. We struck a real bonanza in Biologist Jim.

Jim's big break into scientific circles came when his constant snooping on a strip of Lake Merritt turned up a rare crustacean that was usually covered except during winter floods. Jim's find represented a radical extension of this tiny shrimp's known distribution. Specimens reached a world-recognized marine invertebrate authority, who promptly named the subspecies for Jim. I called on his expertise occasionally when new forms of seaweed, marine invertebrate pollution, or the mistaken practices of city agencies threatened the health and eco-balance of the lake.

Jim's outstanding performance for the naturalist program came once each summer when I drafted him as co-leader for a popular "Tidepool Trip" on a nearby public ocean beach. If you ever conducted from fifty to a hundred people, from preschoolers

211

to grandparents, across the slippery rocks at low tide, you can appreciate this. The likelihood of accidents is so high that I'd risk it only once a season for the general public, and, somehow, we always lucked out. There were other junior helpers, and some real tidepool students, but it was Jim who splashed from pool to pool to identify a strange seaweed here, a minute crab or mollusk there, and it was Jim who reviewed and summarized the various finds when the tidepool snoopers and bewildered amateurs reassembled on the beach. Jim's only handicap was his low voice which made it difficult to locate him among the clusters of eager people around the pools.

When Jim earned his B.A. degree and joined the staff of the California Academy of Sciences as assistant marine biologist, we were all very happy and proud of him. But this didn't fulfill his ultimate ambitions, and after awhile he resigned to reenter the university to work for a Ph.D. degree. Jim never severed his ties with Lake Merritt and his early sponsors. Recently he gave me an autographed copy of a manual of Pacific Coast marine life which he had co-authored.

The "Student Department" I shared with the Oakland Public Museum in the early 1950's differed in that it provided some exciting experiences for a group of six or eight young naturalists. Exciting is really a mild term, for they had some daring teenage boys in command. Take Mike, for example. But first I must tell how they got started.

Alice Mulford and the six-foot boa

When Alice Mulford became curator of the venerable Oakland Public Museum * in the late 1940's, she decided that there must be new life, a new look, and youth. She pushed around the old furniture and antiques to make room for live animal exhibits and for new educational services for children. "What a callous, irresponsible treatment of those precious old pieces," the older museum hands whispered to themselves as they packed more relics of the Gay Nineties up to the attic. But Curator Mulford stubbornly held to her new course.

Boys and girls, even teenagers, came of their own volition. The old musty lecture hall, which had long served as storage space,

* A new Oakland Museum costing ten million dollars opened in 1969 on a site about two blocks from the original Oakland Public Museum. This museum is limited to California displays of natural science, history, and art. A part of the old museum has been preserved as an historic monument, the Camron-Stanford House.

suddenly came alive with animal cases and bird cages. Local television and radio stations took notice of this new look in the museum and invited Miss Mulford and her gang to appear on programs.

Alice Mulford soon found herself involved in the most intimate ways with some of those wild pets. Like the time when she
reluctantly agreed to transport a rattlesnake and a boa constrictor
from Mike's home to the museum to give them a temporary home.
It seems, as Alice recalls it, that Mike's father had arbitrarily ordered his son to clear the house of most of his pets—and particularly of all snakes. Mike's homemade cages containing the rattlesnake
and the six-foot boa were carefully loaded into the trunk compartment of Alice's car for the short trip to the museum. "They're
snake-proof cages, Miss Mulford, and I've got good locks on them,"
Mike had assured her.

There was a stop for another errand en route, and Alice
insisted on lifting the trunk lid to check the live cargo. Her lurking
suspicions were confirmed. There was no boa in the cage! Mike's
supreme confidence in himself must have been shaken as he helped
Alice search her car for the escapee. It was nowhere to be found,
although they could spot no possible route of escape. After examining every cranny and feeling the seat cushions, they closed the
lid, and continued to the museum. They had attracted quite a few
curious passersby where they were parked, and neither Mike nor
Alice really wanted a news story on this event.

The snake was safely placed in temporary quarters at the
museum. For several days Alice carefully rolled up all windows
and locked her car. She even refused rides to certain employees
and friends—inventing pretexts for herself. Neither she nor Mike
had dared disclose to the "museum ladies" what had really happened. Then Alice noticed an odd bulge in the upholstery of the
car near the back window. She felt cautiously. It felt just like a six-
foot snake. She summoned Mike and the two conspirators working
quietly ripped a hole in the upholstery and extracted the reptile.
The boa was unperturbed and quite oblivious to all the turmoil it
had caused, but I'm sure this is still a vivid experience to both
Mike and Alice.

But Mike and his special "club" of budding naturalists sought
greater discoveries and adventures. One or two of them owned
rickety jalopies, so the "club" ranged far afield to bring in more
animals. One such venture lured these young scientists to Mexico.
The deserts and the West Coast offered exotic snakes and lizards,

and the exciting possibility of glimpsing monkeys, parrots, an ocelot, a jagarundi, or a jaguar in a jungle setting. The warm blue waters of the Gulf tempted the scuba divers among them.

The museum had no funds or resources for such a daring venture, but a sponsor provided a four-wheel drive pickup truck for their big 1952 expedition, which lasted six weeks. Camping gear, collecting paraphernalia, film, and groceries were amassed from many sources and funds. Ready cash for gasoline and incidentals was extremely limited. So was the boys' working Spanish vocabulary.

But the guardian angel who hovers over boys on field trips invariably interceded and provided. The caravan broke down on a mountain on a stormy night; they ran out of food and money; they suffered from malaria as well as Montezuma's revenge. But the young adventurers surmounted all setbacks. The boys returned from this and from three subsequent Mexican safaris with iguanas and lesser reptiles, insect collections, and incalculable stores of experience and understanding. Many a tourist and many a friendly Mexican native had lent their hands and hearts in moments of need. Several parents who had fumed and argued and predicted disaster for the first safari gradually relaxed and accepted these jaunts as part of the risks of rearing young naturalists.

Mike's museum movie

Collecting, study, and exhibiting were still not enough for this restless group of boys. Self-appointed leader Mike was the first to conceive the great idea of making a movie. It would not only portray the activities of the boys and their pets, but it would also emphasize the talents of Curator Alice Mulford and her staff who had brought new life to the creaky old museum. There would be some real spooky shots, with the narrow "secret" stairways, the cramped attic festooned with models in gowns of yesteryear, mounted sea lions and pelicans, and what have you. Miss Mulford cooperated enthusiastically. Producer Mike and his ever-eager helpers came up with some ingenious themes and angles, and within a few months, a unique film production was well on its way.

Then a completely unforeseen event interrupted completion of this screen epic. In fact, it threw the entire student department into a panic. Curator Mulford announced she was getting married. She would be leaving very soon to live with her future husband,

John McKenzie, at Fort Ross, where John served as the State Historical Monument curator. Nobody could give assurance that the next museum curator would want to play host to these lively boys and their troublesome animals.

The student department scouted a possible future home at the nearby Snow Museum and at the new Rotary Natural Science Center, which had just opened that September of 1953. The Center lacked space for some of their activities and for collection storage, but it needed boy-power and display ideas. I agreed that the boys could hold some after-school and evening meetings at the Center and that, in return, they would design and build some wall panel displays. A veteran scouter and nature buff, Fred Barnes, agreed to co-sponsor their meetings and programs.

Mike's film-production ambitions continued unabated. Late one afternoon, he phoned from somewhere nearby. He had a very special and urgent request. (Most of Mike's requests were urgent.) "Mr. Covel, can we bring Sisky over to your place for some special shots? They won't let us take them at the museum, and we've got to get them because we have to return Sisky tomorrow." I hesitated since Sisky was a full-grown cougar. Mike and the gang had borrowed this big pussycat from an animal dealer who sponsored some of the boys' activities. Sisky and I had met previously. I thought he was an exceptionally well-behaved cougar, but I had reason to be apprehensive of this animal's role in one of Mike's scripts.

"Bring him over," I agreed, "but you can't do anything with him inside the Center until we close at 5 o'clock." At least, I thought, we'll protect the visiting public even if we do lose some furnishings or part of a boy.

Mike parked his jalopy in front of the Center. Along with him and Sisky were helpers Jim and Leroy. The boys brought Sisky inside, and Mike briefed me on the script. It was wild — as I'd feared.

"What we've got to get, Mr. Covel, is some good sequences of Sisky snarling and then charging."

I asked how they planned to accomplish such a feat since Sisky seemed to be about as wild as Aunt Martha's tabby cat.

"Well, we've got these raw steaks," Mike explained, pointing to a large package held by Jim. "Sisky hasn't eaten since yesterday, and he's got to get excited when he sees these. But we won't let him have any 'till we get our shots."

We all proceeded to the Back Room which at that time hadn't been finished off with displays. Sisky trotted along meekly, still unaware of his part in the script. The boys set up a pair of flood lamps. The movie camera was carefully focused on the far end of the room where Sisky stood with his collar and leash removed. Director Mike got behind the camera and ordered Leroy to show Sisky the meat which Leroy held gingerly in his hand covered with a heavy animal handler's glove. Sisky opened his jaws wide, licked his chops, and then contentedly emitted a sort of purr. "No good," yelled Mike in disgust. "You've got to get him to charge after it. When he starts forward, get yourself off camera fast."

I couldn't take any more of this. I expressed my disapproval and left the room. It would look bad for the park naturalist to be a party to this venture if a boy lost his hand.

An hour later, Sisky was led back to the car, but the boys didn't appear too happy over the results of their cougar filming. "If it doesn't look good when I screen it, we'll shoot it all over again someday when Sisky is hungrier," Mike said.

I was wondering just how much a tame cougar could take. Would all of Sisky's repressed emotions suddenly boil over? Would he wipe out a few customers in his proprietor's pet store, or maybe Mike and his daring film company? I happened to look inside Mike's car where Sisky was being coaxed into the back seat. It was a shambles of torn and chewed-up upholstery. Sisky had already vented all his frustrations on the seat cushions!

The student department boys didn't remain active as a group too long after the cougar-filming episode. The demands of college, the draft, and going steady weaned them away. Were the trials, the little disappointments, and the extra time invested by their various sponsors really worthwhile? A little research on the careers of several of these boys disclosed the following.

After a brave fling at producing a Western-type movie, Mike did make it to Hollywood as a production technician. As far as we know he is still gainfully employed in the motion picture industry. Art graduated from college and became a script and song writer for radio. Jim is a professor on the faculty of a northwestern university. John is a staff entomologist at a large museum in New England. Leroy, an electronics engineer, builds equipment for cosmic ray research, but his photography experience with Mike and the Student Department served him well. While attending college, he was a

216

field cameraman for a local television station, and would frequently appear at the Duck Pond seeking newsreel shots.

Boys have played such prominent parts in this story that you might conclude that there was little room for girls as junior naturalists or little opportunity for them later as "career women" in this field. But the naturalist field had its women libbers years ago.

Sister Mary Lorraine

Among the junior recruits at the Rotary Natural Science Center was Dawnita Duck, an enthusiastic teenage girl. She came with her brother Bill from the old Oakland Public Museum when a change of administration gradually excluded their "junior zoo."

At home, Dawnita and her brother received ample support and encouragement in their wild animal pet exploits. The family was fairly prosperous and could indulge young naturalists' whims. They didn't exactly welcome the boa constrictor their daughter brought home, but they took it in stride. A major crisis did occur during one of the family vacation trips when the boa was boarded with friends. In their anxiety to keep the pet warm and comfy, they exposed it to excessive heat, and a well roasted snake passed to its happy hunting ground.

Dawnita dropped out of the nature center volunteer corps when she reached high school. A number of years later, I received a letter from a Catholic Sisters retreat. It was signed "Sister Mary Lorraine," but in parentheses she had added "Your friend Dawnita." Sister Lorraine was soliciting animals. The Sisters' retreat had extensive grounds and a pond which needed animation by large and lively fowl. A pair of Mute swans would be ideal. Did we have some spares? I would have liked to please Sister Lorraine and the rest of the sisters, but we never did have enough swans to give away.

Some time later Sister Lorraine telephoned that she and other sisters were bringing a bus load of their students to Lakeside Park to see the birds. Could they have a guided tour? It was slightly disconcerting to greet our one-time girl helper as a Catholic sister in traditional habit. But Sister Lorraine radiated understanding and empathy as she introduced snakes and small animals to her pupils.

Since that visit Sister Lorraine has served in many rural communities from California to Texas. At each place she has gathered

217

a small collection of local animals for the children she taught. It is evident that her early experience in the Student Department and at the Natural Science Center will serve her a lifetime, and her early devotion to nature has been incorporated into her devotion to the church.

Did you ever think of the volunteer program of a nature center as a refuge or rehabilitation center for frustrated women? We have found this to be a fact and have reaped many benefits from it, but I don't mean to imply that *all* female recruits have been lovelorn women.

Deanna's search for equal opportunity

Deanna asked if she could be a full-time volunteer aide at the Rotary Natural Science Center. She was a plain, somewhat masculine type in her early twenties with a pleasant manner and considerable confidence when she spoke of her professional background in zoology. She had worked for a nature center in the East but had encountered some difficulties with the director and had decided to return to her folks in Oakland. She hoped to find a position with a new nature center which was soon to open in one of the San Francisco Bay cities.

Deanna proved to be one of our happiest finds. She was trained and willing to do almost anything assigned to her. She even initiated a few new display ideas and carried them out. Since the Science Center never rated a staff preparator, a volunteer who would do things like this was a real asset.

After several months, the new nature center got off the ground. A well-organized community effort raised the funds and Deanna was hired as the director. Although we practically cried when she left, we all wished her well in her new position.

Deanna's new job entailed exhibit preparation, guiding visiting classes, handling correspondence and telephone calls, and, on some occasions, feeding, watering and cleaning the small animal pens. Her "staff" consisted of a part-time helper and a number of volunteers of various ages and abilities. Her salary for directing or doing this complex array of daily tasks was a mere stipend. Anyone would have to be dedicated or, in popular parlance, "a little crazy" to take on such a commitment in these days of the forty-hour week, time-and-a-half for overtime, and numerous fringe benefits. But Deanna took this in stride and never complained about the workload. She frequently stopped by the Science Center to discuss her experiences, and a few problems such as getting enough help and money to finish installations.

We saw less and less of Deanna and presumed that things were smoothing out at her nature center. Then one day she appeared looking completely crushed and bewildered. If she had been more feminine, she would have been sobbing. The society behind the new nature center had decided to hire a male director. He was slightly older than Deanna, a fellow with a charming personality and a convincing line. Deanna would be welcome to stay as his assistant.

This was a bitter pill for Deanna. She had quite a streak of pride and a sense of justice so she had decided to quit the job and go back to school to complete the requirements for a teacher's credential. We had to agree this might be the best course for her. We even hoped that Deanna might return to help us for awhile, but about this time she stopped in to introduce an older man, a fellow who seemed completely enamoured of her. It seemed that we might have underrated her feminine appeal, because they were going steady.

The next news of Deanna announced that she had a teaching position in another western state. It was a little country school, but she didn't seem to mind. Miles of wild southwest country alive with reptiles and other wildlife would surround her new home, and we got the idea that this adoring follower was going along. We never heard much from her, a letter or two and a card, but we sincerely hoped this deserving woman had found happiness in her new environment and new life.

The girl from Missouri

Nancy came to the Center in early summer and announced that she wanted to be a junior naturalist aide. She was from Missouri and was spending the summer with a relative living in Oakland, close to Lake Merritt.

This eager teenager carried out the routine break-in chores— changing rodent cages, feeding meal worms to lizards, and helping the animalkeeper with daily food preparation—all with punctuality and thoroughness. She would even sort the delicate wildflowers and arrange them on the display table. This was enough to convince

219

me she was capable of performing the duties of a first-class aide. She was also kind and gracious to visitors of all ages, and her Missouri accent was most delightful.

There was little doubt that Nancy could qualify for that most demanding and coveted job—helping the naturalists with the day-camp nature shows. This role demanded precise teamwork in such delicate phases as protecting the animal pets from too many eager hands and handing the right animal performer to the naturalist at just the right time. The day camp assistant could also expect to give short, extemporaneous animal introductions when the naturalist needed a break.

The first day camp was a real test of Nancy's tact, patience, and adaptability under trying circumstances. Two hundred youngsters were gathered from many parts of Oakland. Scores of boys and girls from the city's ghetto had never before been exposed to the "big woods." They yelled and screamed and stomped and jostled to keep up their courage.

"Whatcha got? Got any snakes with ya? Can we hold a snake? You got a skunk? Does it stink? What's in that box?" These and a hundred other questions were flung at Nancy as she helped set up the animals in a little amphitheater. Many a teenager would have given short answers to some of these grimy-faced urchins besieging us, but Nancy was a model of patience and understanding.

This performance was repeated an hour later where one hundred and fifty children belonging to a church summer camp awaited us. This camp hadn't built a log amphitheater so we faced the added problem of keeping the youngsters in the front rows from reaching out to touch the animal pets. But the show went off without trouble.

It was Boys' Week at the next camp and the boys were somewhat startled to see an attractive girl arriving to help the naturalist. The only female ordinarily permitted in this week-long, live-in camp was the cook, but this situation didn't faze Nancy as she took over her assignment of demonstrating the snakes.

Nancy grew more adept and knowledgeable, and she also grew on the naturalist staff until we came to dread the end of the summer, when we would lose her services and her cheerful presence. She returned to Missouri at the end of those ten exciting weeks, but we were luckier than we deserved. Back she came the

220

next June to stay in Oakland and to spend another season as "that girl naturalist aide."

Nancy's circumstances changed so that she had to stay in Missouri. Occasionally we received a wistful letter from her, then correspondence dropped to a card and a note at Christmas. A few years later, Nancy wrote of her marriage. This was followed in due time by an announcement that she had started her own family. Then she wrote that they had moved to another state, and she learned that the city to which they had moved had no nature center or naturalist-teacher. She was trying to get the city to establish such a center. In fact she would gladly operate it! This was our protégée—lighting the lamps for nature appreciation in her community.

In subsequent years, a succession of enthusiastic girl volunteer naturalist aides lightened our tasks and brightened our center. They cared for the animals, introduced the harmless snakes to wide-eyed children and parents, patiently stood by while tortoise, iguana, or fawn exercised on park lawns, expertly coped with vexing telephone calls, and tidied up the office and library. Dianne Blackman served faithfully for years, then supplied her future replacement by patiently giving on-the-job training to her younger sister, Dee.

Public reaction to both boy and girl naturalists was fascinating to watch. Adults and children alike seemed to be thrilled as much by the knowledge and technique of the volunteer aide as by the animal shown. You can understand why these young nature types we adopted, encouraged, and sponsored over the years have brought us so much pride and satisfaction. There have been mistakes and heartbreaks along the way, and inestimable amounts of patience and coaching required with all of them. But it all paid off in the satisfaction of having shaped and guided the lives of numerous young people, and sometimes a little glory reflected on us all when our candidates came in at the finish.

Will the practice of accepting eager, serious youngsters as volunteers or junior docents for junior museums, nature centers, and public zoos survive the resistance of department heads and city attorneys who fear liability suits—or from directors or staff who dislike the extra effort necessary to train and supervise the "juniors"? Such resistance must be overcome or an unknown number of potential future naturalists and inspired teachers will be lost to America.

Recently the young volunteers serving two quasi-public children's zoos were banished by insurance company decrees after one accidental animal bite. Our legal system, certain avaricious lawyers, and "give-away juries" are largely to blame for this turn-off of juvenile help. This relates to our comments elsewhere on the disappearance of trees to climb, creeks, bushes, and weed patches to explore in parks, schools, and playgrounds and to the overprotection of urban youth today from natural hazards.

Juvenile volunteers in a governmental agency can be covered by workmen's compensation under California law if the employing agency formally requests such coverage. Nevertheless, under new interpretations of the laws of tort, a regular employee, supervisor, or the agency may be sued for damages if a volunteer, a visitor, or participant is injured through gross carelessness or neglect of the employee or supervisors.

Will you, Mom and Dad, help to give your child the opportunity? Will you, director, curator, or supervisor, make the effort and take the risks? The amount of training and supervision of boy and girl helpers will vary according to age and responsibility but is always critical. However, the achievement of our "naturalist aides" convince me that it is likely to be a most rewarding investment.

Afterword

My many exciting, rewarding years as a park naturalist or *interpreter,* as we are known nowadays, were also motivated by a feeling that a special privilege or mission had been given to me. Most of my fellow naturalists or interpreters that I've met, listened to, or followed afield, were motivated or dedicated to a degree all too rare in modern working society. Whether our followers regarded us as humanized Smokey Bears, "nature men," nature women" or "ecology freaks," they have followed, or sat and listened to us. Even their sometimes restless or disruptive children have returned as appreciative adults and brought their offspring to the "ranger" or interpreter.

When we preached conservation, or ecology and environmental awareness in those earlier years we often felt like missionaries in a backward culture. It is a rewarding measure of success today that so many Americans, including politicians and government office holders, recognize these problems and issues. That hundreds of thousands of Americans belong to organizations like the National Audubon Society, Sierra Club, National Wildlife Federation and a host of others with similar objectives is a healthy and encouraging trend. But the understanding and support of millions of other citizens at all economic and social levels is crucial, and they must be activists in our cause if future American urbanites are to enjoy experiences like those described in this volume.

Early retirement and increased leisure will lead more Americans to open space seeking contact with green things and wildlife. Opportunities to discover "nature next door" will be as vital as those offered by state and national parks, forests and wilderness. Many more interpreters of these resources must be trained and engaged, more environmental or visitors' centers dedicated, if these people and their children are to appreciate and use wisely their precious natural heritage.

Index

225